ONE
to
FIVE

One Shortcut Recipe Transformed into Five Easy Dishes

RYAN SCOTT

Oxmoor
House®

To the most amazing ladies in my life—my loving mother Pat, my beautiful wife Lesley, and then there's Wes ☺ (you know I had to go there, gurrrrl)! Love you all so much.

Published by Oxmoor House, an imprint of Time Inc. Books
225 Liberty Street, New York, NY 10281

Writer: Tamara Palmer
Senior Editor: Betty Wong
Editor: Meredith L. Butcher
Project Editor: Lacie Pinyan
Designers: Maribeth Jones, Olivia Pierce
Photographers: Iain Bagwell, Jennifer Causey, Greg DuPree, Thomas J. Story
Prop Stylists: Kay Clarke, Lindsey Lower, Leila Nichols, Mindi Shapiro, Claire Spollen
Prop Coordinator: Jessica Baude
Food Stylists: Victoria E. Cox, Margaret Monroe Dickey, Karin Shinto, Catherine Crowell Steele
Recipe Testers: Jiselle Basile, Mark Driskill, Paige Grandjean, Emily Nabors Hall, Pam Lolley, Robby Melvin, Callie Nash, Karen Rankin, Deb Wise
Assistant Production Manager: Diane Rose Keener
Associate Project Manager: Hillary Leary
Copy Editors: Jacqueline Giovanelli, Sarah Scheffel
Proofreader: Adrienne Davis
Indexer: Mary Ann Laurens
Fellows: Kyle Grace Mills, Mallory Short

ISBN-13: 978-0-8487-4777-0

ISBN-10: 0-8487-4777-1

Library of Congress Control Number: 2016948459

First Edition 2016

Printed in the United States of America

10 9 8 7 6 5 4 3 2 1

Time Inc. Books products may be purchased for business or promotional use. For information on bulk purchases, please contact Christi Crowley in the Special Sales Department at (845) 895-9858.

We welcome your comments and suggestions about Time Inc. Books.

Please write to us at:

Time Inc. Books
Attention: Book Editors
P.O. Box 62310
Tampa, Florida 33662-2310

CONTENTS

FOREWORD

Ryan Scott has been cooking up a storm on my daytime television show for years. Whenever he stops by, we know we're in for big laughs and great food. He first won over our viewers' hearts with his recipe for Mac-and-Cheese Spring Rolls and that was just the beginning of a delicious friendship. Ryan's recipes are always accessible, affordable, and most importantly, super tasty. Now, he's making mealtime a whole lot easier with his new book *One to Five*.

As the queen of "30-Minute Meals," I'm with Ryan when it comes to getting dinner on the table fast! If you think you don't have anything in the house to cook supper with, let Ryan share his foolproof plan for stocking your freezer and pantry so the kitchen is always open. I've always loved the concept of taking one main ingredient and rolling it over into a ton of tasty meals. Not sure what to do with your leftover broccoli? Check out Ryan's Broccamole! Whether you're looking for snacks for the kids, recipes for your game-day food fest, or a romantic date-night dinner, Ryan's new book covers all the bases. I always say, "Anybody can make a reservation, but if you really want to show someone you care, a home-cooked meal is the way to go." Ryan, too, believes in the power of food and how it can bring people together.

There's a reason I gave him the nickname "Great Scott"....
His "One to Five" concept is so good, I give it a 10!

– Rachael Ray

INTRODUCTION

When it comes to cooking at home, if I can't prep it, cook it, and sit down to eat it in an hour or less, I don't want to do it. It's just that simple.

I've spent more than eighteen years cooking professionally and working in the restaurant business. I've been a line cook, worked with world-renowned chefs, and now lead a growing restaurant group, but when I'm at work, I'm still the guy running around washing pots, executing, and taking out the trash. So when I'm at home, I prefer to spend my time with my wife, Lesley, our families, friends, and especially our dogs, Pumpkin and Teddy, who can often be found glued to the kitchen floor while we're cooking.

I learned to cook from my mother, "Mama Pat." When I was growing up, she worked many jobs, but still managed to put a home-cooked meal on the table every night. We were a working-class family living in suburban California, and there were many years when money was tight. She would transform a pound of ground beef into recipes that are still some of my favorite go-to's today. It was those recipes that have influenced my cooking the most; you'll see touches of what I learned from her, my Nana Cleda, and Grandma Lena throughout the recipes in this book.

It was pretty clear at an early age that working with food was my destiny; there's a picture of me as a boy in the bathtub with a measuring cup that makes me laugh every time I see it. When I turned eleven, my parents were convinced that cooking was in my future because I asked for a food dehydrator for my birthday. I was obsessed with watching the inventor, Ron Popeil, describe it for hours on TV!

I still have that dehydrator sitting in my office today. Those were the early days of food television and Martin Yan, Graham Kerr, Charlie Trotter, and Paul Prudhomme were my idols.

One of my happiest memories of my Grandma Lena is of her making biscuits paired with Jimmy Dean sausage and gravy. Grandpa Charles, a pastor, would wake up and make himself a cup of Sanka coffee in the microwave (yep, you heard me right!), and together, we would watch my grandma roll out the most beautiful, uniform, perfectly round biscuits I'd ever seen using an empty S&W green bean can as a dough cutter.

Years later, when I asked my grandma for her recipe, she laughed and told me her secret recipe was no secret at all—her biscuits were simply made from Bisquick. I was shocked! For nearly three decades, I had been convinced that she possessed a secret recipe or had a mysterious ingredient that was responsible for those flaky biscuits of perfection. That pivotal moment helped me realize that good food doesn't always need to be made from scratch. It was the love that she put into making those biscuits for her family that made them so special— and how we used to devour them, smothered in sausage and gravy!

This cookbook will teach you how to make some items (such as my versatile ranch dressing) from scratch, but also how to take advantage of precooked ingredients and already-made foods to achieve big flavors. At home, I rely on products that are easy to find in almost any supermarket in the U.S.: cake mix, canned tuna, microwavable brown rice—ingredients to simplify cooking and save time. As you cook your way through *One to Five,* I hope that my recipes will help you develop your own shortcut dishes, without compromising on taste. You're going to learn both the confidence and skills to create quick, easy, stretch-a-dollar meals that you'll want to make again and again.

The philosophy behind *One to Five* is so easy you will want to kiss me: Name a simple ingredient, and I'll give you a quick way to prepare it that can be transformed into five great dishes to serve throughout the week. The key is to keep your freezer and pantry stocked with basics that you can combine with fresh ingredients and spices so you can whip up an elevated meal at the drop of a hat. Whether you are living life at a hundred miles an hour or you're someone who likes to take things slow, regardless of how much you love cooking—this book is for you. *One to Five* will make getting meals on the table simple—stupid simple—just follow my time-saving shortcuts and tips for repurposing one recipe or ingredient to make the most out of each one. Think of me as your new best cooking friend.

Food for me has always been about family, friends, and memories. Once you are gathered around the table to share a meal, everything else fades away: the day's worries, work stress, tomorrow's to-do list. All of these concerns take a backseat to living in the moment, connecting with family and friends who are passing a delicious dish around your table. That summarizes my whole approach to cooking at home: Keep it simple, get to the table, and enjoy your meal.

xox,

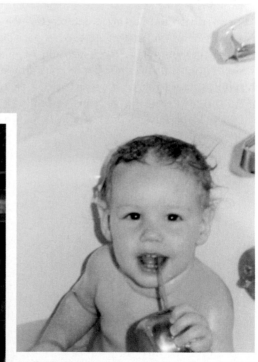

STAPLES: STOCKING YOUR FRIDGE, FREEZER, AND PANTRY

You can do without many things, but you can't do without food! If you nail down your staples—the tools you'll use to cook and the ingredients you'll always keep in your fridge, freezer, pantry shelves, and drawers—you'll become a versatile chef who's always ready for action. By keeping your kitchen well stocked, you'll be economizing while simultaneously broadening the quality and diversity of your day-to-day meals.

Expanding your repertoire by picking up one new ingredient when you shop can take your food to a whole new level. It doesn't need to have a fancy name or expensive price tag: Just grab something like tahini (sesame paste) or curry paste in a tube (see descriptions on page 14). Don't be afraid to drop an extra five dollars here and there to try something new!

Below I've described all of my favorite staples—the ingredients that get me ready to make the recipes in this cookbook, and so many other snacks and meals. Don't feel pressured to buy everything in this list at once; instead use it as a guide that will help you grow your cooking skills. I will be honest and admit that items such as beef jerky, Sour Patch Kids, pretzel thins, and booze are also among my pantry staples. But that's just me—they are optional for you!

THE FRIDGE

Beer: Did you know you can use this as a fantastic meat tenderizer, marinade, or base for a fluffy frying batter? In my house, I am usually double-fisting beers—one for cooking and one for drinking.

Better Than Bouillon: Forget those old-fashioned bouillon cubes and keep a jar of Better Than Bouillon paste in the fridge; it comes in flavors that range from beef to chicken to vegetable. It's a MSG-free intensifier for soups and sauces, as well as an amazing base for marinades and rubs.

Biscuit dough: Head to page 28 to see how easily you can transform refrigerated biscuit dough into appetizers, desserts,

and even the main event, all of which will have people begging for the recipe.

Crumbled blue cheese and feta cheese: It's good to have a cheese with a lot of flavor on hand. If you're new to these cheeses, they can smell overwhelming, but when used with other ingredients they will heighten the flavors of your food.

Unsalted butter: An emulsifier and a binder, butter makes quick sauces. You should be in control of the salt in your dishes, especially when baking, which is why I always use unsalted butter.

Capers: A bastardized child of the culinary world that needs to be brought back to the forefront, capers make for a big flavor addition to your sauces, brines, salads (like Kale Caesar on page 79) and seafood (including Danny's Lemon-Pepper Scampi on page 178). When people ask me what the trick is in a dish, it's often the juice that the capers are stored in!

Cheddar: Buy this in a block, not preshredded; the dishes that call for shredded Cheddar will taste a lot better if you shred it yourself. It also makes a nice snack when you buy it this way; just slice and munch. By the way, true Cheddar is not orange; that's a dye. Cheddar is white.

Dijon mustard: You won't know how good this ingredient is until you start using it regularly. It's not just an emulsifier for your vinaigrettes, it's also a zesty rub and the unexpected kick in the best barbecue sauces. I love Dijon!

Eggs: This is an inexpensive protein that can feed a whole family when you're in a bind (or even when you're not). You'll find easy and delicious ideas for hard-boiled eggs for breakfast, lunch, and dinner beginning on page 19. Whoever said having breakfast for dinner was wrong? It's a fast, easy, and cheap way to get a meal on the table.

Fish sauce: Usually a combination of anchovies, salt, and water, fish sauce is an incredible condiment that makes many Asian dishes shine; there's just no substitute for it. If you've never tried cooking with it, consider it one of your

experiments. It can seem intimidating when you taste it on its own, but trust me, it's another story when you add it to dishes!

Garlic: I prefer garlic paste above all other forms of garlic, but I also like to keep minced garlic in a tub or jar on hand—just stay away from varieties packed in oil, as they oxidize quickly.

Ginger paste: Ginger can be hard to chop and clean, so I'm a fan of using ginger paste. Using the tube form gives you instant ginger zing ASAP.

Herb pastes: I rely heavily on garlic and ginger pastes for the recipes in this book (they're wonderful time-savers), but I also make sure I've got basil and chili pastes on hand. They're a smart crutch that you won't mind leaning on for marinades, rubs, and other quick fixes.

Pickled jalapeños: I used to be wary of jalapeño peppers until I learned that they don't just offer heat—they give you sweet, savory, bitter, and salty flavors as well. They're one of my go-to ingredients in this book and you shouldn't be intimidated by them; embrace the canned jalapeño!

Ketchup: Don't overlook this condiment! It can be the base for a barbecue sauce and the key to a nice crust on a meatloaf. Thousand Island dressing is nothing without ketchup, after all.

Mayonnaise: This condiment can be taken in so many directions. Use it on chili, rub it on tuna (you heard me right), or bake a mayo-tossed chicken breast—it keeps proteins so moist.

Whole milk: Keep milk around for more than just your cereal. It's useful as a cooking liquid or as a base for dressings.

Italian parsley: Also sold as flat-leaf parsley, it's got such a vibrant flavor that it can withstand a whirl in the food processor. Mince with garlic and lemon zest to rub on pork roast or beef top round, or use it with lemon juice to dress fish.

Pepperoncinis: I'm addicted to pepperoncinis, either sliced or whole. They contribute a little hidden kick of acid that bumps up the flavor of so many dishes or salads!

Pickles: Think outside the pickle jar. Dill pickles contain acid, just like capers and pepperoncinis; utilize the juice as an alternative brine for fried chicken.

Salsa: Find a brand you like with good heat, and add it to ground beef for tacos, to avocados and lemon juice for a quick guacamole, or just enjoy it with tortilla chips.

Sour cream: Perfect for creamy dressings or as a soup topper, sour cream can also cut the heat in spicy dishes in no time flat. This is a key ingredient in my Chickpea, Asparagus, and Feta Dip (page 219). Stir it into Mama Pat's Meat Sauce (page 137), pour the sauce over some egg noodles, and you've got an easy stroganoff.

Yogurt: It's a good meat tenderizer or a substitute for mayonnaise in a low-calorie salad dressing. For versatility,

your best bet is the plain unsweetened kind; I'm a fan of the nonfat one from Fage.

THE FREEZER

Frozen berry medley: It's perfect for throwing into jams, sauces, vinaigrettes, or desserts. You'll learn how boiling this dollar-stretching ingredient can quickly turn it into a versatile condiment, scene-stealing side dish, or amazing potluck meal.

Frozen bread or breadcrumbs: See page 202 for all sorts of ideas for transforming your frozen bread (or stale bread from the pantry) into wonderful meals.

Frozen microwaveable brown rice: Star of the section beginning on page 180, bags of brown rice that are ready to zap in your microwave are useful for a lot more than a serving on the side. With this convenient product on hand, appetizers, entrées, and desserts are less than an hour away!

Puff pastry sheets: Making your own puff pastry is time consuming and labor intensive, but the frozen kind is versatile enough to use in sweet or savory applications, from pastries to pot pies.

Frozen shrimp: Turn to page 169 to see all the delicious dishes you'll be making from a simple bag of cooked and peeled frozen shrimp. This versatile protein is a good replacement for more expensive ingredients and will help you get a quick meal ready in a flash.

Frozen vegetables: Buy single varieties of vegetables such as broccoli, green beans, butternut squash, corn, and spinach to use as a filler or a stretcher to bulk up dishes. You'll even find a whole section in this book on using frozen corn (see page 158).

THE PANTRY

Almonds: These can be used in both sweet and savory dishes. Almonds are good blanched, sliced, slivered, or whole, and you can freeze them and use them for (almost) forever.

Almond milk: Because so many people are lactose intolerant or follow a dairy-free or vegan diet, I like to keep almond milk on hand to accommodate my guests. Utilizing almond milk as a substitute for cow's milk can add a new dimension to a dish.

Baking powder and baking soda: Baking powder is a mix of baking soda, a dry acid (like cream of tartar), and cornstarch and is used as a leavener; you'll see it in recipes for cookies and cakes. Baking soda is a base; it gives off carbon dioxide when exposed to heat and creates gas bubbles in batter, making it lift and rise. I use it in potato cakes at my restaurant Market & Rye because it makes them fluffy and keeps them from becoming gluey.

Bay leaves: They never get their due credit, but when added to a stew or sauce, dried bay leaves will completely change a dish.

People are used to removing them before serving, but they're also perfect when crumbled and put in a crust or in stuffing.

Bisquick: I already shared the story of how I learned that Bisquick was the secret to my grandmother's incredible biscuits. It never leaves my pantry now.

Canned black beans: If you're going to keep any cans of beans in your pantry, let them be black beans. They can play in every single game, from savory cakes to stuffings to the best-darned puree in the world—pair it with scrambled eggs, crispy tortillas, and more.

Black pepper: You may notice that I don't include pepper in all of the dishes in this book; that's because I consider it an ingredient, not an accompaniment. But when pepper is needed, it's a superstar that takes center stage, as in my Brown Sugar–Black Pepper Bacon (page 113).

Seasoned breadcrumbs and panko: Already toasted and in possession of a great herb flavor, seasoned breadcrumbs save you a lot of steps, though this book will also teach you how to make your own breadcrumbs (page 203). Panko (large, flaky, Japanese-style breadcrumbs) make for a crunchier and lighter batter, so I like to keep those stocked as well—in fact, I use them more frequently than seasoned breadcrumbs.

Brown sugar: Of course brown sugar is a staple for all kinds of desserts, but did you know that brown sugar and fresh thyme can heighten the flavors of a clam chowder? Think of it as a secret weapon even when you're not using it to bake cookies.

Cake mix: Store-bought mix can be a fantastic baking shortcut for a whole range of treats, including the churros, cookies, and other ideas you'll find starting on page 236.

Cannellini beans: These white Italian kidney beans are creamy, protein-packed nuggets that make an effective binder for savory cakes, like my Broccoli-Cheddar Ranch Burgers (page 49). They have an amazing texture that holds up well when you drop them in a dish near the end of the cooking time.

Chicken stock: I recommend keeping a box of chicken stock in the refrigerator versus a can in the pantry if you're using stock a lot. Whether you're making gravies, sauces, or braises, even inexpensive dishes will be richer, deeper, and have more body when you add chicken stock instead of water.

Chickpeas: One of the only ingredients out there that doesn't taste like the can it's sold in, chickpeas are probably the best ingredient you'll ever serve straight from a can. Flip to page 212 to see how the oft-forgotten garbanzo takes center stage in a variety of mains and sides.

Chocolate: Semisweet or bittersweet chocolate is good for cooking, baking, and devouring by the fistfuls.

Cinnamon: Not just a spice for Christmastime, cinnamon is also your ally when you're making Indian-inspired dishes, popovers, pies, and strudels. I buy ground cinnamon as well as sticks to put in tea or jars of tomato jam.

Canned coconut milk: Lactose-free and vegan, coconut milk has a stereotype of being sweet, but it really isn't (cream of coconut is the sweet one). Thin it out and add it to stews and sauces, or use it in pancakes instead of milk; coconut milk always makes a really good dish even better.

Nonstick cooking spray: If you don't have nonstick pans, this helps you cook lighter and saves on calories. I use it when making cornbread, tamales, eggs—all kinds of dishes. Nonstick spray shouldn't replace oil altogether in your cooking, but if you're looking to cut back on fat, it can be a smart alternative.

Ground coriander: Amazing with beef, fish, or black beans, this is a must-have spice that you'll find yourself using more and more as you cook your way through the recipes in this book.

Corn Flakes: I think of Corn Flakes as way more than a cereal. In fact, we sell thousands of Corn Flake–crusted fried chicken sandwiches every week at Market & Rye. Use them like you'd use panko flakes to batter and fry up something awesome, or as that special crunch in a meatloaf. Adding Corn Flakes to any of your cookie recipes will take them over the top.

Cornmeal or corn muffin mix: Yes, you can use it for cornbread, but you can also make johnnycakes. The mix is a shortcut to tamale pie and fritters. Just keep a box around; you'll find it's a time-saver!

Cornstarch: I frequently use cornstarch in baking, especially for cakes and pancakes. The end result is creamier and more buttery on the inside. It's also great in savory applications, like my 7UP Battered Salt-and-Pepper Cauliflower (page 56).

Canned cranberry sauce: Most people just buy this ingredient once a year, for Thanksgiving, but you can use it for so much more. Try it in barbecue sauce! You'll be amazed at how tasty it is.

Cream of mushroom soup: Great for stews and casseroles or in comforting recipes like Lesley's Biscuit Chicken Turnovers (page 101), this canned soup gives you an already finished sauce to work with—you don't even have to chop and cook the mushrooms!

Cumin: Whole or ground, cumin is often that unidentifiable flavor people always ask about in just about any dish with an ethnic flair. Toasting it takes its flavor up a notch. If cumin isn't already a standby in your kitchen, I'd like to see this spice become part of your repertoire.

All-purpose flour: AP flour is useful as more than just an ingredient for baking; it's also a common binder used in a wide variety of recipes in this book. You can also dust your cutting board with all-purpose flour to help keep your workspace clean and tidy.

Wondra flour: A partially cooked flour that doesn't clump up in batter and makes crispy coatings. Wondra is almost foolproof in cooking or baking. Be sure to fully cook it before consuming.

Canned green chiles: Already roasted, peeled, and diced, these are a wondrous step-saver, and their sweetness and meatiness makes them a perfect introductory chile pepper for people who are afraid of heat. Add canned green chiles to enchiladas, stews, and a variety of appetizers.

Hot sauce: I love hot sauce. Period. Make one yourself using my Carrot Hot Sauce (page 68) or buy a bottle (or six), and keep Sriracha, tapitio, or my fave—Tabasco—on hand to add a little heat and flavor to everything. I love them all, but Tabasco is my go-to for cooking because of its sweet heat, acid, and all over deliciousness.

Kidney beans: An inexpensive ingredient you don't have to cook, soak, or braise to use, canned kidney beans can eally shine when you add them to salads—just drain them and toss in.

Lemons: Fresh lemon juice is a frequently used ingredient in this book because it heightens, extends, and brings vibrancy to a wide variety of dishes. It's my go-to for finishing fried chicken and fish, and in my household it's key to the dressings and marinades I use every day.

Limes: Lemons are always my first choice, even for guacamole. But if you don't have any on hand, use limes squeezed on top of chips or salsa or Mexican food.

Maple syrup: Not just for your pancakes, think of maple syrup as an ingredient you can use in savory applications as well. Drizzle it on top of oven-roasted sweet potatoes or use it for charring vegetables.

Nutmeg: Another spice that usually gets relegated to the winter holidays, nutmeg should be considered a year-round spice. It goes wonderfully with pasta, sausage, or broccoli.

Oils: I like to keep vegetable, canola, and soybean oils on hand as neutral fats for cooking. I use olive oil primarily for dressings and finishing rather than cooking; it can be expensive, so saving it for finishing dishes allows you to extend it farther.

Kalamata olives: I love briny, rich Kalamata olives in salads, dressings, roasted with chickpeas or broccoli, or to elevate any vegetable.

Red onion: This is your go-to onion for recipes where you're pickling, but they also have their place in raw or braised dishes. They cook down sweetly and even go surprisingly well with strawberries—yep, you heard me!

Yellow onion: White onions have a bite, while yellow onions have a sweeter flavor overall. I prefer them in most of my recipes that call for onions.

Pancake mix: Not just for pancakes, pancake mix can coat deep-fried peanut butter and jelly sandwiches or make memorable corn dogs. Think outside the box with this versatile starter.

Paprika: Another add-in that can bring a dish up to the next level, paprika should be in every kitchen. It lends chili a smoky depth of flavor, or you can sprinkle it in the flour mix when you're dredging chicken for frying.

Pastas: I keep a variety of dried pastas in my pantry for quick meals. My favorites are elbows and penne—both bake and reheat well and absorb all of the flavors in the sauce—as well as no-boil pasta sheets, like the ones I use for my EZ Cottage Lasagna (page 141).

Peanut butter: A good emulsifier that never goes bad, peanut butter tastes great on just about anything. It can make your sauce killer or your smoothies and vinaigrettes extra amazing. I also enjoy a spoonful straight up for a quick snack.

Potato chips: A sister to Corn Flakes, potato chips can be a surprise ingredient in desserts, or as a crust for mac and cheese or chicken.

Pretzel sticks: Crush and roll pork chops in pretzel dust for a schnitzel, or use them in my Kitchen Sink Cookies (page 247).

Quinoa: A complete protein, quinoa cooks quickly and brings life to salads, stuffings, and sides. Spend the money for this whole grain! It's a Scott house staple.

Ranch powder: You can obviously make ranch dressing using ranch powder, but you can also use it as a seasoning in a dredge for chicken or pork chops, or in dips.

Roasted red bell peppers: I don't personally like fresh red bell peppers, but I do keep jars of roasted bell peppers in the pantry for an added twist to marinades, salsas, or salads, like my Tuna Pasta Salad (page 199).

Red chile flakes: People get scared because they think chile flakes are just for making food hot, but they also can balance out the acid and salt in your dishes. Don't hesitate to sprinkle on some chile flakes; they can change the way you cook.

Ritz Crackers: These crackers are ideal for making quick appetizers on the fly—decking them out with ham, cheese, and a pickled ingredient is always a reliable formula. And the crumbs are great for topping casseroles or mac and cheese, or for a unique sweet and salty piecrust.

Soy sauce: Super-concentrated, soy sauce will give your dishes an intense finish. Try it in barbecue sauce and stir-fries as your source for salt. It gets saltier as it reduces, so add the soy after you've turned off the heat. I also use light soy sauce for vinaigrettes at my house. It's a "what did you add to this dish?" kind of ingredient.

Taco seasoning packet: Use a brand that includes a chili note and add it to stews, chicken enchiladas, chili, ground beef, or ground turkey. With this seasoning packet on hand, you won't have to keep so many individual spices in your cabinet.

Tahini: A roasted sesame paste, tahini is perfect for marinades and dredging. You can also mix it with yogurt or sour cream to use as a cooling agent or sauce for spicy dishes. Please splurge and buy this! Keep it refrigerated after you open it.

Thai curry paste: I choose green curry paste over powder to avoid the dryness the powder can impart. The addition of this paste makes any quick fish, pork, or beef dish taste exotic. Try my Green Curry Cauliflower "Rice" (page 63), and you'll see how Thai curry paste works its magic.

Canned plum tomatoes: Stock up on a good-quality brand of canned tomatoes—both whole and diced. They're a year-round go-to for chili, sauces, chutneys, soups, stews, braises, and more.

Canned tuna: Find a dolphin-safe brand (such as StarKist) that you like, and then hop over to page 190 to see how this humble and super-affordable protein will enable you to make a wide variety of dishes. It's already cooked and ready to go!

Vanilla extract: Just a few drops of vanilla can make a box cake or pancake mix taste glam, or use it as a secret flavor catalyst in super-tasty carrots with maple syrup.

Vegetable broth: Veggie broth is time consuming to make. Choose a can of it if you're not using a lot, or use a box if you are. Cook veggies in vegetable broth not chicken stock to keep them 100 percent vegetarian.

Vinegars: I keep apple cider vinegar, red wine vinegar, and rice wine vinegar in my pantry for a wide range of applications, from sweet to savory to pickled dishes. Apple cider vinegar is also useful for taking care of sore throats!

White wine: Not just for drinking, white wine elevates blond sauces, such as the one in Danny's Lemon-Pepper Scampi (page 178), as well as for chicken and fish sauces and for deglazing a pan. But go ahead and enjoy a glass, too.

Worcestershire sauce: A key component to robust marinades and braises, barbecue sauce doesn't taste like barbecue sauce without Worcestershire. I also add it to my Beefy French Dip-Onion Soup (page 153).

ESSENTIAL KITCHEN TOOLS

Blender and food processor: If you are going to invest in two kitchen appliances, they should be a high-power blender and a decent food processor. Your food processor doesn't have to be an expensive one to help you with prepping ingredients, but you'll save money by shredding cheeses and chopping your own veggies and fruits instead of buying them already prepped, which always costs more.

Can opener: Many ingredients in this cookbook come from a can, so you need a can opener to open them. Manual or fancy automatic, it's your choice.

Colander: A colander is not only handy for straining ingredients, it's useful for washing fruits, vegetables, and herbs. Choose a mesh colander rather than a plastic one so that you can strain hot as well as cool foods safely.

Dutch oven: A large deep pot with a tight-fitting lid is an invaluable tool in the kitchen and a worthwhile investment. You can do way more than you'd think in this one-pot-meal wonder, from baking bread to making stews.

Microplane grater: Stop buying that processed Parmesan cheese in the green can and discover the wonders of freshly and finely grated Parm with the help of this little tool. It's also handy for zesting lemons and grating garlic, fresh ginger, and any other type of hard cheese. Trust me, a Microplane grater will make a number of dishes in the book even more amazing.

Kitchen scissors/shears: You'd be surprised how much you need scissors in the kitchen. A good pair of kitchen shears will cut through the hardest things with ease, including chicken or fish bones.

Ladle: Not only is a ladle handy for making stock or serving up soup for dinner, it's the tool you need when it's critical to skim the fat off of a risotto or a braise.

Rolling pin: I'm a baker at heart, so I love having a rolling pin within easy reach. It's useful for crushing things (like ice in a zip-top bag) or to evenly roll out anything. You don't need the type with the handles, just get a wooden dowel.

Nonstick sauté pan, stock pot, and sheet pans: These are basic tools that will be in constant use in your kitchen. My 10-inch pan is the most-used tool in our house—if you're starting with no pans at all, this is your best point of entry.

Slotted spoon: For making meatballs, poaching eggs or chicken, or boiling anything, a slotted spoon helps you raise and lower the ingredients into your cooking liquid.

Spatula: Flip burgers, grill meat or veggies, slice lasagna, or get the crust off of a mac and cheese—the spatula can do it all.

Steamer: Look for a retractable metal steamer that will fit in your Dutch oven as well as in a 6-inch pot with a lid. It's the best way to steam your veggies.

Vegetable peeler: A wide vegetable peeler is best for removing the tough outer skins of carrots and broccoli and makes a cheap stand-in for those fancy vegetable-ribbon makers that they try to sell you on TV.

Wooden spoon: I swear by this classic cooking tool, which will get you down into the corners of your pot so you can reach the fond—all those scrumptious brown bits that can be hard to access otherwise.

STOCK THE DRAWERS

Aluminum foil: The dull side absorbs heat so the shiny, reflective side of the foil should always be facing in toward what you're cooking. Your dish may not reach the intended internal temperature if the reflective side is facing out toward your heat source.

Parchment paper: A helpful tool when baking both savory and sweet recipes, parchment holds fish or meats in packets and lines pans for cookies, brownies, and cakes for easy release.

Plastic bags: We use zip-top bags for all sorts of jobs in our kitchen, including freezing stock, saving carrot peels, and keeping damp napkin-wrapped herbs fresh.

Plastic wrap: While major manufacturers of plastic wrap don't advise that you use it in the oven, you can use it to cover food when steaming or cooking it in the microwave, and of course, to save your leftovers in the refrigerator before you reuse them in another recipe.

EGGS

The humble and hearty egg became a really good friend of mine when I started pricing out food as a restaurant owner. I think it's often overlooked as the quick, simple, and delicious protein that it is, so it's time to shout it out for the star that it can be! Here you will learn how boiling this dollar-stretching, incredible edible can quickly and easily turn it into a versatile condiment, devilishly scene-stealing side dishes and sandwiches, and a full scene-stealing potluck meal.

Once these are cooked, you have about five days to use them. My method for making them is hard to mess up, but please make sure the water comes to a full boil before adding the eggs. Store cooked eggs unpeeled in the refrigerator until ready to use.

FOOLPROOF HARD-BOILED EGGS

HANDS-ON: 10 MINUTES   TOTAL TIME: 32 MINUTES   MAKES 12

12 large eggs

Ice cubes

1 Fill a large saucepan or Dutch oven with enough water to cover the eggs. Bring the water to a full boil. Add the eggs, return the water almost to a boil, and cook for 6 minutes. Turn off the heat, and let the eggs sit for 6 minutes.

2 Pour out half of the water, and cover the eggs with ice cubes. Let the eggs chill for 10 to 15 minutes. Drain.

For easy shell removal, roll a hard-boiled egg on the bottom of the kitchen sink to slightly crack the shell all over. Submerge it in water as you peel off the shell with your fingers.

1

12 hard-boiled eggs (page 19), peeled

⅔ cup mayonnaise

2 teaspoons Dijon mustard

2 teaspoons brined caper juice (from jar)

2 teaspoons fresh lemon juice

1 teaspoon kosher salt

Dash of hot sauce, such as Tabasco

¼ cup chopped fresh chives, for topping

Paprika, for garnish

The quintessential go-to appetizer of the ages, deviled eggs are easy to make and never fail to impress. They have become something we are known for at my restaurant Market & Rye. Star chefs around the country, from Geoffrey Zakarian to Tyler Florence, have elevated them to the stratosphere. And now here's my take. Consider reserving a cup of the egg yolk filling to use in a deviled egg salad sandwich (page 25) the next day.

RYAN'S DEVILED EGGS

HANDS-ON: 20 MINUTES   TOTAL TIME: 20 MINUTES
MAKES 24 DEVILED EGG HALVES

Cut the eggs in half lengthwise. Carefully remove the egg yolks, and add them to the bowl of a food processor. Set aside the egg white halves. Add the mayonnaise, mustard, caper juice, lemon juice, salt, and hot sauce to the egg yolks in the food processor, and process until smooth. Spoon or pipe the egg yolk mixture into each egg white half. Sprinkle with the chopped chives, and garnish with the paprika.

If you prefer a thicker egg filling, reduce the mayonnaise by one-third.

To pipe the filling, spoon the egg yolk mixture into a zip-top plastic freezer bag. Snip one of the bottom corners off the bag to make a small hole. Pipe the mixture into the egg white halves.

EXTRA CREDIT!

Get creative with toppings!
Try sprinkling with my Brown
Sugar–Black Pepper Bacon
(page 113), crispy salami,
jalapeño peppers and cheese,
or even fried oysters.

2

6 hard-boiled eggs (page 19), peeled

2 tablespoons fresh lemon juice

1 tablespoon red wine vinegar

1 tablespoon Dijon mustard

1 tablespoon brined caper juice
(from jar)

2 dashes of hot sauce, such as Tabasco

1 teaspoon black pepper

½ teaspoon kosher salt

1 cup extra-virgin olive oil

½ cup finely chopped red onion

¼ cup chopped dill pickles

¼ cup finely chopped fresh flat-leaf
parsley

¼ cup finely chopped scallions

1 tablespoon brined capers, drained
and chopped

When I worked at the high-end restaurant Gary Danko in San Francisco, then–sous chef Brandon Sharp (now the executive chef at Solbar in Napa Valley) really opened my eyes to new ways to make amazing things out of what other chefs might consider scraps. This dressing is inspired by his sauce *gribiche*, an egg dressing that's fabulous with salmon, grilled veggies, salads, and more.

EGG DRESSING

HANDS-ON: 10 MINUTES   TOTAL TIME: 10 MINUTES
MAKES ABOUT 3 ½ CUPS

1 Pulse 4 of the eggs with the lemon juice, vinegar, mustard, caper juice, hot sauce, pepper, and salt in a food processor, just until the eggs are chopped. With the processor running, slowly drizzle the oil through the food chute until smooth. Transfer to a medium bowl.

2 Roughly chop the remaining 2 eggs. Stir the chopped eggs, red onion, pickles, parsley, scallions, and capers into the dressing.

3

Welcome to pickled eggs on overdrive! These couldn't be simpler to prepare, but you do want to make sure you have a clean, preferably new, glass container to use. They're a great make-ahead snack because you can refrigerate them for up to 2 weeks.

JALAPEÑO PICKLED EGGS

HANDS-ON: 5 MINUTES   TOTAL TIME: 6 MINUTES, PLUS CHILLING
MAKES 12 PICKLED EGGS

1 Combine 2 cups water, the vinegar, garlic paste, salt, pickling spice, sugar, and bay leaves in a stockpot; bring to a boil over medium-high. Remove from the heat.

2 Combine the onion and jalapeños in a clean, airtight 2-liter glass container. Carefully place the eggs in the container, and then add the vinegar mixture, making sure the eggs are completely submerged. Chill in the refrigerator for 12 to 24 hours before eating.

2 cups water

1 ½ cups red wine vinegar

1 tablespoon refrigerated garlic paste (from tube)

1 tablespoon kosher salt

1 tablespoon pickling spice

½ tablespoon sugar

2 bay leaves

1 white onion, slivered

2 jalapeño chiles, sliced crosswise

12 hard-boiled eggs (page 19), peeled

EXTRA CREDIT!

Make these sandwiches Southwestern by adding a can of diced green chiles and pickled jalapeño peppers, or Korean by swapping chopped kimchee for the chili paste.

Kudos to my sous chef, Vanesa Sanchez, who has worked with me for almost a decade. Customers were constantly asking for an egg salad sandwich since we're so well known for our deviled eggs. She came up with this sandwich, and now we can't take it off the menu!

RYAN'S DEVILED EGG SALAD SANDWICHES

HANDS-ON: 20 MINUTES   TOTAL TIME: 20 MINUTES   SERVES 4

1 Cut the eggs in half lengthwise. Remove the egg yolks, and add them to the bowl of a food processor. Roughly chop the egg whites, and set them aside. Add the mayonnaise, mustard, caper juice, lemon juice, chili paste, salt, and hot sauce to the egg yolks in the food processor, and process until smooth. Transfer the mixture to a large bowl; stir in the chopped egg whites and cilantro.

2 Place the lettuce leaves on one side of 4 bread slices; top each with the egg salad mixture (don't be afraid to get really messy) and 1 tomato slice. Cover with the remaining bread slices.

Be careful not to overchop the cilantro; it will lose body and flavor the more you bruise it.

12 hard-boiled eggs (page 19), peeled

⅔ cup mayonnaise

2 teaspoons Dijon mustard

2 teaspoons brined caper juice (from jar)

2 teaspoons fresh lemon juice

2 teaspoons Asian chili paste or chili garlic sauce, such as Huy Fong

½ teaspoon kosher salt

Dash of hot sauce, such as Tabasco

¼ cup loosely packed roughly chopped fresh cilantro leaves

8 to 12 Bibb lettuce leaves

8 slices of bread (your choice—white, whole-wheat, or potato bread; something with pull that will give you some crunch), toasted

1 medium tomato, sliced into 4 (½-inch-thick) slices and salted

5

HOMEMADE RANCH (makes 5 cups)

2 tablespoons finely chopped red onion

2 teaspoons red wine vinegar

2 teaspoons fresh lemon juice

2 teaspoons sugar

2 teaspoons onion powder

1 ½ teaspoons kosher salt

1 teaspoon black pepper

3 cups mayonnaise

2 cups buttermilk

¼ cup finely chopped fresh flat-leaf parsley

¼ cup finely chopped fresh chives

SALAD

1 head iceberg lettuce, chopped

¾ cup green beans

¾ cup marinated artichoke hearts, drained

¾ cup shredded carrots

¾ cup chopped tomatoes

¾ cup Broccolini tops

3 hard-boiled eggs (page 19), peeled and sliced crosswise

¾ cup shredded Brussels sprouts

¾ cup chopped pitted black olives

¾ cup shredded red beets

1 small English cucumber, cut into strips

¾ cup crumbled blue cheese

Growing up, my mom was a big fan of using what we had to make meals. If something was missing, we didn't run to the store to get it; we made do instead. Don't be frustrated if you don't have all the ingredients I use here—just use what you've got, and you'll end up with an amazing salad that easily serves the family or a dinner party. I use ranch powder frequently in this book, but this is the one time where making ranch dressing from scratch is totally worth it!

MEATLESS KITCHEN SINK COBB SALAD WITH HOMEMADE RANCH

HANDS-ON: 25 MINUTES   TOTAL TIME: 25 MINUTES   SERVES 8

1 Prepare the homemade ranch: Combine the red onion, vinegar, and lemon juice in a large bowl, and let stand 5 minutes. (This helps to remove the raw onion bite.) Whisk in the sugar, onion powder, salt, and pepper. Whisk in the mayonnaise until incorporated. While whisking, slowly add the buttermilk until blended; add the parsley and chives. (Note: The dressing will keep without the herbs for 2 to 3 weeks in the refrigerator.)

2 Assemble the salad: Plate this family style on a large serving platter. Put the lettuce on the bottom, and then create color-alternating rows. Try this order from left to right: green beans, artichoke hearts, carrots, tomatoes, Broccolini, eggs, Brussels sprouts, black olives, beets, and cucumber. Sprinkle the blue cheese over the top. Serve the salad with 2 cups of the dressing; reserve the remaining dressing to use as needed.

If you're working with whole vegetables that need to be shredded in a food processor, put the beets through last so they don't turn everything red.

BISCUIT DOUGH

Remember when I said it's perfectly okay to use smart shortcuts to get a meal made quickly? Think of those ready-to-bake biscuits you have in the fridge or freezer as a super-universal dough. Unlike phyllo or pie dough, biscuit dough isn't fragile and it's very forgiving. It's also a versatile friend for appetizers, entrées, sweets, and savories, as you'll see when you get it popping! While it's pretty easy to open biscuit dough containers, you still might want to move slowly to avoid any potential messes.

START WITH: REFRIGERATED BISCUIT DOUGH

1 EGGS FLORENTINE IN A HOLE
2 PEANUT BUTTER AND JELLY TIME
3 GARLIC-BASIL BISCUIT BOMBS
4 SAN FRANCISCO GIANTS PIZZA BALLS
5 CARAMEL-APPLE-BLUEBERRY CRISP

Eggs Florentine, poached eggs with spinach and Hollandaise Sauce, was one of the first dishes I learned how to make in college. Now that Lesley and I have family and friends over all the time, I've adapted the recipe to suit our breakfast crowds. Turkey bacon lightens up this dish, while chard makes it a little earthier.

EGGS FLORENTINE IN A HOLE

HANDS-ON: 20 MINUTES   TOTAL TIME: 1 HOUR   SERVES 12

1 Preheat the oven to 375°F. Cook the turkey bacon in a large skillet over medium-high until golden brown and crispy, 6 to 8 minutes. Transfer to a plate lined with paper towels to drain.

2 Add the oil to the skillet, and heat over medium-high. Add the onion, mushrooms, salt, pepper, and chile flakes, and cook until the onions start to caramelize, about 7 minutes. Add the chard, and cook until tender, about 7 minutes. (Add a little water if the mixture gets too dry.) Add the spinach, and cook until it wilts, about 30 seconds. Using a slotted spoon, transfer the mixture to a medium bowl.

3 Lightly grease a 12-cup muffin pan with nonstick cooking spray. Separate the biscuit dough. Using a rolling pin, roll out each biscuit on a lightly floured surface until the biscuit triples in size (about 5 inches in diameter). Place the dough rounds in the muffin pan, pressing onto the sides and bottom of the cups so that the edges fold over onto the top of the muffin pan. Break each bacon slice in half, and place 2 halves in each muffin cup, forming an X shape. Top each with 1 tablespoon of the chard-spinach mixture. Put the muffin pan on an aluminum foil–lined rimmed baking sheet, and bake until the dough starts to brown, about 20 minutes.

4 Separate the eggs into bowls. Whisk the egg whites lightly until combined. Remove the muffin pan from the oven, and put 1 egg yolk in each muffin cup. Top with just enough of the whites to fill each cup; discard any remaining whites. Divide the mozzarella evenly among the cups. Return to the oven, and bake until the egg whites are just set and the dough is a deep golden brown, about 15 minutes. (The yolks likely will be runny. For firmer yolks, bake 5 minutes more.) Serve hot or at room temperature.

12 slices turkey bacon

2 tablespoons vegetable oil

1 cup finely chopped yellow onion

1 cup chopped cremini mushrooms

1 teaspoon kosher salt

1 teaspoon black pepper

⅛ teaspoon red chile flakes

3 cups loosely packed roughly chopped Swiss chard leaves

3 cups loosely packed roughly chopped spinach

1½ (16.3-ounce) packages refrigerated biscuit dough

12 large eggs

⅓ cup shredded mozzarella cheese

2

1 cup fresh blackberries

¾ cup blackberry jam

3 tablespoons fresh lemon juice

¾ cup confectioners' sugar

1 cup creamy peanut butter

6 tablespoons heavy cream

1 cup dry-roasted salted peanuts

6 cups vegetable oil

1 (16.3-ounce) package
refrigerated biscuit dough

I'm hooked on this place in San Francisco called Bob's Donuts that people like to go to late at night (occasionally when they're drunk), but I rarely splurge on it because I'm the guy who gains weight in two seconds. Their crumb donuts and peanut butter and jelly sandwiches are both serious vices of mine, so this is my collision of two addictions together in one epic quick treat. These are why I wake up and wonder why I can't see my feet.

PEANUT BUTTER AND JELLY TIME

**HANDS-ON: 10 MINUTES   TOTAL TIME: 15 MINUTES
MAKES 8 DOUGHNUTS**

1 Place the blackberries in a medium bowl; roughly mash them with a potato masher. Stir in the jam, lemon juice, and ½ cup of the confectioners' sugar; set aside. Stir together the peanut butter, cream, and remaining ¼ cup confectioners' sugar in a separate bowl.

2 Process the peanuts in a food processor until finely chopped. Transfer them to a large bowl.

3 Heat the oil in a deep fryer until a candy thermometer reads 350°F. (If you don't have a deep fryer, you can use a Dutch oven.) Separate the biscuit dough. Working in batches, fry the dough, turning once, until deep golden brown and cooked through, about 2 minutes per side. Transfer to a plate lined with paper towels to drain for 1 minute. Roll the hot doughnuts in the crushed peanuts.

4 Using a chopstick or wooden skewer, poke a hole into the side of each doughnut, wiggling the chopstick from side to side to create a ¼-inch hole. Transfer the peanut butter mixture to a large zip-top plastic freezer bag. Snip one corner off the bag. Pipe the peanut butter mixture into each doughnut until it almost bursts and the mixture begins to ooze from the side of the doughnut. Sprinkle the doughnuts with any remaining crushed peanuts. Serve with the jam mixture for dipping.

EXTRA CREDIT!

Try varying the fruits for dipping! Consider strawberries, blueberries, or red grapes.

EXTRA CREDIT!

Serve with ranch dressing or warm marinara sauce for dipping.

My savory take on Monkey Bread can serve as a one-pan appetizer or side dish. I guarantee it's going to disappear quickly if you serve it straight from the pan, so I'll leave it up to you whether to present it as one or to ration it out carefully.

GARLIC-BASIL BISCUIT BOMBS

HANDS-ON: 10 MINUTES   TOTAL TIME: 30 MINUTES   MAKES 32 PIECES

Preheat the oven to 400°F. Stir together the basil, oil, garlic paste, salt, and pepper in a medium-sized nonstick ovenproof skillet. Roll the dough pieces in the basil mixture to coat. Arrange them in a single layer so they are touching and cover the bottom of the skillet. Bake for 10 minutes. Remove from the oven, and sprinkle with the Parmesan. Return to the oven, and bake until golden brown, about 10 minutes. Garnish with the fresh basil leaves.

Don't worry if the pieces aren't uniform; the biscuits are more fun to pull apart when you have irregular shapes.

½ cup chopped fresh basil

¼ cup extra-virgin olive oil

2 teaspoons refrigerated garlic paste (from tube)

½ teaspoon kosher salt

½ teaspoon black pepper

1 (16.3-ounce) package refrigerated biscuit dough, biscuits separated and cut into quarters

1 cup freshly grated Parmesan cheese (about 4 ounces)

Fresh basil leaves, for garnish (optional)

4

4 ounces mild ground pork sausage, such as Jimmy Dean

1 cup chopped cremini mushrooms

1 cup diced red onion

1 tablespoon vegetable oil

2 cups shredded mozzarella cheese (8 ounces)

½ cup chopped pepperoni slices

¼ cup roughly chopped fresh basil

¼ cup drained and chopped jarred roasted red peppers

¾ teaspoon dried oregano

1 (16.3-ounce) package refrigerated biscuit dough

1 large egg, beaten

½ cup freshly grated Parmesan cheese (about 2 ounces)

¼ teaspoon black pepper

2 cups marinara sauce, warmed

Looking for an easy alternative to pizza night? These golden orbs are almost the size of baseballs, which reminds me of my home team, and they freeze beautifully.

SAN FRANCISCO GIANTS PIZZA BALLS

HANDS-ON: 15 MINUTES   TOTAL TIME: 40 MINUTES
MAKES 8 PIZZA BALLS

1 Preheat the oven to 375°F. Cook the sausage in a medium skillet over medium-high until crumbly and crispy, about 5 minutes. Transfer to a plate lined with paper towels to drain, reserving drippings in the skillet. Add the mushrooms, onion, and oil to the skillet, and cook until the vegetables are softened, about 5 minutes. Transfer the mushroom mixture to a medium bowl, and add the sausage, mozzarella, pepperoni, basil, red peppers, and ½ teaspoon of the oregano; stir to combine.

2 Separate the biscuit dough. Using a rolling pin, roll out each biscuit on a lightly floured surface until the biscuit triples in size (about 5 inches in diameter). Brush the edges of the dough rounds with a small amount of the beaten egg; scoop ¼ cup of the sausage mixture into the center of each biscuit. Gather the dough edges around the sausage mixture, forming a purse, and press to seal. Roll gently on the cutting board to form a ball. Repeat with the remaining balls.

3 Lightly grease a baking sheet with nonstick cooking spray. Put the pizza balls on the sheet, seam sides down, and gently roll them to lightly coat with cooking spray. Brush the pizza balls with the remaining beaten egg. Top each ball with about 1 tablespoon Parmesan. Sprinkle them with the black pepper and the remaining ¼ teaspoon oregano. Bake until the dough is golden brown and fully cooked, 22 to 25 minutes. Serve with the warm marinara sauce.

EXTRA CREDIT!

Serve with ice cream while
the crisp is still warm.

Ordinary crisps just can't compare to what you're about to prepare. You'll love this spin on cinnamon rolls after you taste them and discover what a snap they are to assemble.

CARAMEL-APPLE-BLUEBERRY CRISP

HANDS-ON: 30 MINUTES   TOTAL TIME: 50 MINUTES   SERVES 12

1 Preheat the oven to 400°F. Heat the oil in a large nonstick ovenproof skillet over medium-high. Add the apples, and cook until caramelized, about 7 minutes. Transfer to a plate. Add the brown sugar, cream, butter, and salt to the skillet, and whisk to combine. Bring to a boil, stirring occasionally, and stir in the apples, blueberries, walnuts, and apple juice. Cook until the apple mixture is bubbly, about 1 minute. Remove from the heat.

2 Using a rolling pin, roll out the dough on a lightly floured surface into a single sheet, about 12- x 6-inches. Sprinkle the granola evenly over the dough; press gently to adhere it. Roll up the dough from a long side. Slice the rolled dough crosswise into 12 (1-inch-thick) pieces. Turn the dough pieces cut sides up so they look like pinwheels, and press gently to flatten them. Arrange the pinwheels on top of the apple mixture in the skillet so they are touching and cover most of the apple mixture. Brush the dough with the beaten egg. Bake until golden brown, about 20 minutes.

2 tablespoons vegetable oil

4 cups chopped Granny Smith apple (about 3 apples)

1 cup packed light brown sugar

½ cup heavy cream

2 ounces (¼ cup) unsalted butter

1 teaspoon kosher salt

1 cup fresh blueberries

1 cup chopped walnuts

¼ cup apple juice

1 (16.3-ounce) package refrigerated biscuit dough

1 cup granola of your choice

1 large egg, beaten

BROCCOLI

Growing up, I thought of broccoli as an overcooked veggie that looked a little like the bottom of my shoes. I'm sure my dad is reading this cookbook right now, looking for credit, but the only credit I can give him here is that he taught me how not to cook vegetables. If only my dad knew back in 1988 how amazing broccoli can be, maybe I'd be two inches taller today!

People are used to eating just broccoli florets, but the whole vegetable is great. You can trim off those little nubs and leaves if you like, but you are missing out on some potential deliciousness if you do.

STEAMED-AND-SHOCKED BROCCOLI

2 medium heads broccoli with stems, trimmed and split in half lengthwise

Bring a few inches of water to a boil in a large stockpot. Put the broccoli halves in a steamer basket, fanning them out so they cook evenly, and place the steamer in the pot. (Make sure water is boiling before adding broccoli.) Cover and steam until the broccoli is tender, 6 to 7 minutes. Plunge broccoli into a large bowl of ice water to stop the cooking process; let sit 2 to 3 minutes. Drain completely in a colander. Store drained, cooked broccoli for up to 5 days in the refrigerator.

START WITH: STEAMED-AND-SHOCKED BROCCOLI

1 BROCCOLI-ALMOND PESTO
2 BROCCAMOLE
3 BROCCOLI-KALE SLAW
4 BROCCOLI-CHEDDAR RANCH BURGERS
5 BROC-O-TOTS

EXTRA CREDIT!

Use this pesto with mozzarella cheese as a stuffing for chicken or pork chops.

Pesto is an awesome sauce, but it's typically pricey to make because of the inclusion of pine nuts. My version uses the thriftier almond-and-broccoli combo for a stealthy health boost. If your kids don't like broccoli, this is a great way to sneak it in!

BROCCOLI-ALMOND PESTO

HANDS-ON: 10 MINUTES   TOTAL TIME: 10 MINUTES   MAKES 1 ½ CUPS

Chop the broccoli stems, reserving the florets. Process the stems in a food processor until finely chopped. Add the Parmesan, almonds, garlic paste, salt, and hot sauce; process until combined. Add the broccoli florets, spinach, basil, oil, and lemon juice; process until incorporated.

1 medium head broccoli, steamed and shocked (page 43)

2 tablespoons grated fresh Parmesan cheese

2 tablespoons roasted salted almonds

¾ teaspooon refrigerated garlic paste (from tube)

½ teaspoon kosher salt

2 dashes of hot sauce, such as Tabasco

¼ cup firmly packed fresh spinach

¼ cup firmly packed fresh basil leaves

1 tablespoon extra-virgin olive oil

1 tablespoon fresh lemon juice

2

My broccoli-based take on guacamole is an inexpensive alternative to using avocados, which I promise you will not miss here! Serve with chips and salsa or the dipping vehicle of your choice; my wife loves this on toast.

BROCCAMOLE

HANDS-ON: 10 MINUTES   TOTAL TIME: 10 MINUTES   SERVES 6

2 medium heads broccoli, steamed and shocked (page 43)

½ cup roughly chopped scallions

1 jalapeño chile, seeds removed, chopped

¼ cup fresh lemon juice

¼ cup sour cream

2 ounces cream cheese, softened (about ¼ cup)

2 teaspoons garlic powder

1 teaspoon kosher salt

1 teaspoon taco seasoning mix

½ teaspoon ground cumin

½ cup firmly packed fresh cilantro leaves

Chop the broccoli stems, reserving the florets. Process the stems, scallions, and jalapeño in a food processor until finely chopped. Add the lemon juice, sour cream, cream cheese, garlic powder, salt, taco seasoning, and cumin; process until combined. Add the broccoli florets; process until smooth. Add the cilantro; process just until incorporated.

This easy slaw is perfect on its own or as a side for roasted chicken or pork chops. It's also a great way to learn how to incorporate healthy kale into dishes that eaters of all ages will love. This dish can last for days, because when you're working with earthy greens like broccoli and kale, they get better as they sit.

BROCCOLI-KALE SLAW

HANDS-ON: 20 MINUTES   TOTAL TIME: 20 MINUTES   SERVES 6

1 Prepare the dressing: Whisk together all ingredients in a small bowl.

2 Prepare the slaw: Shred the broccoli stems using a box grater, and break up the florets by hand, to equal about 2 cups broccoli total. Toss together the broccoli, kale, carrots, scallions, sunflower seed kernels, and toasted sesame seeds. Add the dressing; toss with your hands or tongs to coat the salad.

Use leftover dressing (about 1 cup) as a raw veggie dip another day.

DRESSING (makes 2 cups)

½ cup mayonnaise

¼ cup rice vinegar

2 tablespoons fresh lemon juice

2 tablespoons sugar

1 ½ teaspoons whole-grain mustard

1 ½ teaspoons Dijon mustard

¼ teaspoon kosher salt

¼ teaspoon black pepper

SLAW

1 medium head broccoli, steamed and shocked (page 43)

2 cups shredded kale (such as lacinato)

1 cup shredded carrots

1 cup finely chopped scallions

¾ cup roasted salted sunflower seed kernels

¼ cup toasted sesame seeds

EXTRA CREDIT!

Crunch it up with toasted quinoa, almonds, or salted cashews.

This recipe was inspired by my deep and undying love of two things: Ranch dressing and broccoli-Cheddar soup. Consider this a mashup of those comforting flavors! Try this as a clever vegetarian alternative.

BROCCOLI-CHEDDAR RANCH BURGERS

HANDS-ON: 30 MINUTES   **TOTAL TIME: 1 HOUR, PLUS CHILLING**   **SERVES 7**

1 Heat 2 teaspoons of the oil in a medium skillet over medium-high; add the onion, and cook until softened, about 2 minutes. Remove from the heat; let cool slightly, about 10 minutes.

2 Stir together the broccoli florets, quinoa, and soup in a large bowl.

3 Process the broccoli stems, onion, beans, ranch dressing mix, garlic powder, cumin, and hot sauce in a food processor until smooth. (If the mixture doesn't come together at first, add a drizzle of warm water—about 2 tablespoons—to get it going.) Add the broccoli stem mixture to the broccoli floret mixture in the bowl; stir to combine. Fold in the Cheddar and breadcrumbs by hand.

4 Using a ¼-cup measure, shape the broccoli mixture into 15 (½-inch-thick) patties. Arrange them in a single layer on a parchment paper-lined baking sheet. Cover with plastic wrap, and chill the patties for 2 to 4 hours. (If you're in a hurry, freeze the patties for 30 minutes.)

5 Heat 2 tablespoons of the oil in a large nonstick skillet over medium-high until shimmering. Add 5 patties in a single layer, and cook, turning once, until golden, about 2 minutes per side. Drain the patties on a plate lined with paper towels. Repeat with the remaining patties, adding 1 tablespoon of the remaining oil per batch.

¼ cup plus 2 teaspoons vegetable oil

½ cup chopped yellow onion

1 medium head broccoli, steamed and shocked (page 43), stems and florets separated and chopped

1 cup cooked quinoa

¼ cup canned cream of broccoli soup

¾ cup canned cannellini beans, drained

1 tablespoon ranch dressing mix, such as Hidden Valley

1 teaspoon garlic powder

½ teaspoon ground cumin

¼ teaspoon hot sauce, such as Tabasco

1 cup shredded Cheddar cheese, (3 ounces)

½ cup Italian-seasoned breadcrumbs

5

I created Broc-O-Tots to handle your (okay, my) tater tot cravings without the potato. Psst—they're another sneaky way to get some veggies into your kids. The deception heightens when you dip them in ketchup!

BROC-O-TOTS

HANDS-ON: 15 MINUTES   TOTAL TIME: 30 MINUTES   MAKES ABOUT 50

2 ½ cups diced steamed and shocked broccoli (page 43)

½ cup diced yellow onion

¾ cup shredded Cheddar cheese, (4 ounces)

2 large eggs, beaten

2 tablespoons ranch dressing mix, such as Hidden Valley

½ teaspoon kosher salt

1 ½ cups fine, dried breadcrumbs

3 tablespoons vegetable oil

Nonstick cooking spray

Ketchup or Sriracha chili sauce, for serving

1 Preheat the oven to 425°F. Process the broccoli and onion in a food processor until finely chopped, about 5 seconds. Transfer to a large bowl. Stir in the Cheddar, eggs, ranch dressing mix, salt, and 1 cup of the breadcrumbs. Let stand for 5 minutes.

2 Sprinkle a thin layer of the remaining ½ cup breadcrumbs onto a work surface. Roll 1 cup broccoli mixture into a ¾-inch-thick rope that is 20 to 24 inches long, pressing mixture together as you go. Repeat with the remaining breadcrumbs and broccoli mixture. Cut the ropes into about 50 (1-inch) tots.

3 Heat 1 tablespoon of the oil in a large nonstick skillet over medium-high. Working in batches, arrange the tots in a single layer in the skillet; cook just until golden on the bottom but not browned, about 1 minute. Repeat the process two times with the remaining oil and tots.

4 Place the tots, unbrowned sides up, 1 inch apart on an aluminum foil-lined baking sheet lightly coated with the cooking spray. Lightly coat the tops of the tots with cooking spray. Bake until crispy, about 15 minutes. Serve with ketchup or Sriracha.

CAULIFLOWER

Like its close cousin broccoli, cauliflower is something I learned to appreciate when I began my career in cooking. I love cauliflower because it can be the lead singer of your show, but it can also play backup and not demand to be Mick Jagger all the time! (Asparagus, I'm looking at you, kid.) A simple steamed and shocked head of cauliflower will yield you a wide range of possibilities, including pickled and fried appetizers, low-carb "rice," and a beautiful baked cauliflower casserole that just may make you turn your back on mac and cheese.

STEAMED-AND-SHOCKED CAULIFLOWER

1 medium to large head of cauliflower

Bring a few inches of water to a boil in a stockpot. Cut out and discard around from the core of the cauliflower head, without loosening any of the florets. Place the cauliflower head, core side down, in a steamer basket over the boiling water. (Make sure the water is at a full boil before adding the cauliflower.) Cover and steam the cauliflower until almost tender, 8 to 10 minutes. Plunge the cauliflower into a large bowl of ice water to stop the cooking process; let it sit for at least 3 minutes. Drain. Store the drained, cooked cauliflower for up to 5 days in the refrigerator.

START WITH: STEAMED-AND-SHOCKED CAULIFLOWER

1. SWEET 'N' HOT PICKLED CAULIFLOWER
2. 7UP BATTERED SALT-AND-PEPPER CAULIFLOWER
3. CAULIFLOWER, BACON, AND JALAPEÑO BAKE WITH RANCH CRUMB TOPPING
4. SRIRACHA, SESAME, AND SCALLION CAULIFLOWER
5. GREEN CURRY CAULIFLOWER "RICE"

These peppy pickles are my take on an old Italian grandma's *giardiniera,* but mine start off nice and sweet before bringing on the heat. Keep them submerged in the pickling liquid in an airtight container, and they'll last for at least two months in your fridge—if you do not eat them all first.

SWEET 'N' HOT PICKLED CAULIFLOWER

HANDS-ON: 10 MINUTES   TOTAL TIME: 6 HOURS   MAKES 8 CUPS

1 Put the sugar, salt, chili paste, garlic paste, pickling spice, chile flakes, 2 cups water, and the vinegar in a large stockpot. Bring to a boil over medium-high, stirring well to combine, and cook for 5 minutes. Add the cauliflower and both bell peppers. Remove from the heat, and let stand, uncovered, for 2 to 6 hours.

2 Pour the pickling liquid, cauliflower, and bell peppers into a large bowl. Make sure the vegetables are fully submerged in the liquid.

3 Put a plate on top of the bowl to create an airtight seal. Chill for 2 to 6 hours, and transfer to an airtight container. Refrigerate for at least 2 months.

I like McCormick pickling spice, which includes cinnamon, allspice, mustard seed, bay leaves, ginger, coriander, and black pepper, among other ingredients.

½ cup sugar

1 ½ tablespoons kosher salt

1 tablespoon refrigerated chili paste (from tube)

1 tablespoon refrigerated garlic paste (from tube)

1 tablespoon pickling spice, wrapped in cheesecloth and tied with kitchen twine

¾ teaspoon red chile flakes

2 cups water

1 cup white wine vinegar

1 medium head cauliflower, steamed and shocked (page 53), cut into 1-inch pieces

1 red bell pepper, chopped

1 green bell pepper, chopped

2

¾ cup instant-blending flour, such as Wondra

½ cup cornstarch

2 teaspoons kosher salt, plus more for serving

2 teaspoons black pepper, plus more for serving

½ teaspoon baking powder

1 cup 7UP

3 large egg whites

8 cups vegetable oil

1 large head cauliflower, steamed and shocked (page 53), cut into bite-sized pieces

EXTRA CREDIT!

Add fresh herbs of your choice to the skillet right before the cauliflower turns golden brown for a simple but powerful flavor enhancer.

My wife and I are big fans of Japanese cuisine—especially tempura vegetables, which are battered and fried. Tempura batter is typically done with rice flour and club soda, but I love the toasted flavor you get from using Wondra, a partially cooked flour that will keep the batter from clumping. The kicker is the lemony zip that comes from 7UP. The two work to create a light and fluffy batter for the cauliflower that you can also use with shrimp or other precooked vegetables such as sweet potatoes, carrots, or zucchini. The world is your batter. Serve with barbecue sauce, ranch dressing, yogurt, or your favorite dip. A squeeze of fresh lemon juice will make the dish even brighter.

7UP BATTERED SALT-AND-PEPPER CAULIFLOWER

HANDS-ON: 20 MINUTES   TOTAL TIME: 20 MINUTES   SERVES 3

1 Whisk together the flour, cornstarch, salt, pepper, and baking powder in a medium bowl. Gradually add the 7UP, gently stirring to combine. Beat the egg whites with an electric mixer on medium speed until fluffy, and fold them into the 7UP mixture. Keep the batter cold in a bowl of ice to maintain fluffiness.

2 Heat the oil in a large skillet over high until a candy thermometer reads 350°F to 375°F. Dip the cauliflower pieces in the batter, and fry, in batches, in the hot oil until golden brown, 1 to 2 minutes. Drain on paper towels, and season liberally with more salt and pepper.

No 7UP? Sub in Sprite, ginger ale, club soda, or even a light beer. To fry at the right temperature, a candy thermometer works great, or you can use a wooden spoon: Stick the handle of the spoon on the bottom of the oil-filled skillet. Bubbles will rise from the bottom of the spoon and try to escape when the oil reaches frying temperature.

I spent a lot of time at my godmother Mara's house when I was a kid. She was all about stretching a dollar and hiding veggies. One of my favorite dishes of hers was a broccoli and cauliflower bake. Here is my homage to Mara. I've updated her classic recipe and spiked it with Cheddar, bacon, and jalapeño.

CAULIFLOWER, BACON, AND JALAPEÑO BAKE WITH RANCH CRUMB TOPPING

HANDS-ON: 20 MINUTES   TOTAL TIME: 1 HOUR 5 MINUTES   SERVES 12

1 Preheat the oven to 425°F. Cook the bacon in a large skillet over medium until crispy, about 10 minutes. Drain the bacon on paper towels, reserving the drippings in the skillet. Chop the bacon, and set aside. Add the onion, the room temperature butter, and the chopped fresh jalapeño to the skillet. Cook over medium until tender, about 6 minutes. Remove from the heat.

2 Stir the flour, salt, and pepper into the onion mixture. Add the milk, both cheeses, the pickled jalapeño, and half of the chopped bacon, and stir until the cheese is melted. Stir in the cauliflower, and transfer to a lightly greased 13- x 9-inch baking dish.

3 Stir together the breadcrumbs, ranch dressing mix, melted butter, and remaining bacon in a medium bowl, and pour over the top of the cauliflower mixture. Bake until golden brown, 45 to 55 minutes.

I've recommended baking at high heat, but you also can cook this casserole slow and low for longer until bubbly in the center, and then crank up the heat at the end until the topping is crunchy. This dish should overflow with goodness, but you don't want to make a mess—so consider placing the baking dish on top of a foil-lined baking sheet before sliding it into the oven.

6 slices bacon

½ medium-sized yellow onion, diced

2 ½ ounces (5 tablespoons) unsalted butter at room temperature, plus 2 tablespoons, melted

1 jalapeño chile, seeds removed, chopped (about 2 tablespoons)

6 tablespoons instant-blending flour, such as Wondra

2 teaspoons kosher salt

1 teaspoon black pepper

3 cups whole milk

2 cups shredded mozzarella cheese (8 ounces)

1 cup shredded Cheddar cheese (4 ounces)

1 tablespoon pickled jalapeño chile, chopped

1 large head cauliflower, steamed and shocked (page 53), chopped

1 cup breadcrumbs from day-old bread

1 cup Italian-seasoned breadcrumbs

1 tablespoon ranch dressing mix, such as Hidden Valley

4

Though it doesn't have the same ingredients, this dish was inspired by the flavors of kung pao chicken and features Sriracha. The sweet and spicy sauce mellows the cauliflower, which can sometimes taste a little earthy. Serve as an appetizer (just add toothpicks!) or an entrée over microwaveable brown rice.

¼ cup soy sauce

¼ cup rice wine vinegar

¼ cup sweetened condensed milk

1 tablespoon Sriracha chili sauce

1 teaspoon refrigerated garlic paste (from tube)

1 teaspoon refrigerated ginger paste (from tube)

1 tablespoon fresh lemon juice

1 ½ cups all-purpose flour

1 cup whole milk

½ teaspoon baking powder

1 medium to large head cauliflower, steamed and shocked (page 53), cut into bite-sized pieces

¼ cup vegetable oil

¼ cup sliced scallions

1 tablespoon toasted sesame seeds

SRIRACHA, SESAME, AND SCALLION CAULIFLOWER

HANDS-ON: 40 MINUTES   TOTAL TIME: 40 MINUTES   SERVES 4 TO 6

1 Stir together soy sauce, vinegar, condensed milk, Sriracha, garlic paste, and ginger paste in a small saucepan. Bring to a boil over medium-high; reduce heat to medium, and simmer, stirring often, until slightly thickened, about 5 minutes. Remove from the heat, and stir in the lemon juice; set aside.

2 Stir together the flour, milk, and baking powder in a medium bowl until a thick batter forms. Dip each cauliflower piece into the batter; shake off the excess, and place the pieces on a wire rack lightly coated with cooking spray.

3 Heat the oil in a large skillet over medium-high until it shimmers. Add cauliflower pieces, in batches, and cook until crispy and browned on all sides, about 4 minutes. Transfer to a plate lined with paper towels to drain.

4 Combine the cauliflower and half of the soy sauce mixture in a large bowl, and toss to coat. Top with the scallions and sesame seeds, and serve with the remaining sauce.

This dish is a nod to my Mama Pat. My mother was a big fan of rice pilaf when we were kids, and my twist on the dish will help you expand your flavor profile in the kitchen. Cauliflower is the perfect vegetable stand-in for rice, and a super-healthy alternative to cooked grains. Green curry paste isn't overpowering; instead, it adds a bright, vibrant element that gives you deep flavor without bringing too much heat.

GREEN CURRY CAULIFLOWER "RICE"

HANDS-ON: 15 MINUTES   TOTAL TIME: 40 MINUTES   SERVES 5

1 Pulse the chopped cauliflower in two batches in a food processor until finely chopped. (Don't worry if you end up with some bigger cauliflower pieces in the mix. It'll still taste great!) Heat the oil in a large skillet over medium; add the onion, salt, and pepper, and cook, stirring occasionally, until the onion is tender, about 7 minutes. Add the curry paste, ginger paste, garlic paste, and chicken soup base, and cook, stirring often, for 1 to 2 minutes.

2 Add the cauliflower "rice" to the onion mixture in the skillet, stirring just until combined. (Do not overmix.) Pat the mixture down in the pan.

3 Cover and reduce the heat to medium-low, and cook until the bottom is browned, 20 to 30 minutes. Remove the lid, and cook, uncovered, for 5 minutes. Fluff the pilaf mixture, and sprinkle with the almonds, scallions, and cilantro.

When cooking onions, pick up a piece and push it against the roof of your mouth. If it disintegrates, it's ready.

1 large head cauliflower, steamed and shocked (page 53), chopped

¼ cup canola oil

1 medium-sized yellow onion, diced

2 teaspoons kosher salt

1 teaspoon black pepper

2 tablespoons green curry paste

2 tablespoons refrigerated ginger paste (from tube)

2 tablespoons refrigerated garlic paste (from tube)

1 teaspoon chicken soup base, such as Better Than Bouillon

½ cup slivered almonds, toasted

½ cup chopped scallions

½ cup loosely packed chopped fresh cilantro leaves

CARROTS

It may surprise you to learn just how adaptable and forgiving carrots can be in the kitchen. Unlike my dogs, Pumpkin and Teddy, they are very obedient and always listen to you. Steam up this inexpensive root vegetable, and you'll be able to take it to unexpected places: use it as the secret ingredient in a sweet and spicy hot sauce, the star of a great salad, a foundation for fresh takes on hummus and latkes, and the hidden healthy base for muffins that are so sweet and moist they almost taste like cupcakes.

STEAMED-AND-SHOCKED CARROTS

10 medium carrots (about 1 pound)

Peel the carrots using a vegetable peeler. Trim off about ½ inch from the bottom and top of each carrot. Bring a few inches of water to a boil in a large stockpot. Arrange the carrots in a steamer basket, and place the steamer in the pot. Cover the pot, and steam the carrots until tender, about 7 minutes. Plunge the carrots into a bowl of ice water; let sit for 2 to 3 minutes to stop the cooking process. Drain. Store the drained, cooked carrots for up to 5 days in the refrigerator.

START WITH: STEAMED-AND-SHOCKED CARROTS

1 CARROT HUMMUS

2 CARROT HOT SAUCE

3 CARROT-GINGER LATKES

4 CHARRED CARROT SALAD WITH HERB DRESSING AND FETA

5 CARROT, CRANBERRY, AND ZUCCHINI MUFFINS

EXTRA CREDIT!
Use my Carrot Hot Sauce
(page 68) instead of Tabasco!

My wife, Lesley, and I usually have about five variations on hummus in our fridge at any given time; I love flavors like roasted garlic and jalapeño hummus. Usually all of these contain garbanzo beans, but I've found that carrots can take their place and really shine.

CARROT HUMMUS

HANDS-ON: 10 MINUTES   TOTAL TIME: 20 MINUTES   MAKES 4 CUPS

1 Heat the canola oil in a medium skillet over medium-low. Add the onion, ginger paste, garlic paste, cumin, salt, and garlic powder, and cook until the onions are translucent, about 5 minutes. Add ½ cup water, and cook 1 minute, stirring occasionally.

2 Process the onion mixture, chopped carrots, olive oil, tahini, lemon juice, and hot sauce in a food processor until smooth. Garnish with toasted sesame seeds, chopped cilantro, and a drizzle of olive oil. Serve with pita chips or even Triscuits!

2 tablespoons canola oil

1 ½ cups diced yellow onion

1 tablespoon refrigerated ginger paste (from tube)

1 tablespoon refrigerated garlic paste (from tube)

2 teaspoons ground cumin

2 teaspoons kosher salt

1 teaspoon garlic powder

½ cup water

10 medium carrots, steamed and shocked (page 65), chopped (about 3 cups)

¾ cup extra-virgin olive oil, plus more for drizzling

½ cup tahini (sesame paste)

¼ cup fresh lemon juice

2 dashes of hot sauce, such as Tabasco

Toasted sesame seeds, for garnish

Chopped fresh cilantro, for garnish

2 tablespoons canola oil

2 cups diced yellow onion

1 jalapeño chile, seeds removed, diced

1 tablespoon refrigerated garlic paste
(from tube)

1 teaspoon red chile flakes

**10 medium carrots, steamed and
shocked (page 65), roughly
chopped (about 3 cups)**

2 cups water

1 cup red wine vinegar

3 tablespoons fresh lemon juice

2 tablespoons sugar

4 teaspoons kosher salt

If you know me, and you've peeked into my fridge, you know
I'm addicted to hot sauce. I even have a hot sauce bar at my
restaurant. While I love heat and spicy food, my guests don't
always share the same preference. So, this rendition is a sweet
and spicy all-purpose hot sauce with a little kick that everyone
can enjoy. Try it on tacos or over scrambled eggs, in a Bloody
Mary, or as a dip for French fries. You'll be surprised how
good it is!

CARROT HOT SAUCE

HANDS-ON: 5 MINUTES   TOTAL TIME: 20 MINUTES   MAKES 5 CUPS

1 Heat the oil in a medium skillet over medium-high. Add the onion,
jalapeño, and garlic paste, and cook until the onions are translucent,
about 7 minutes. Add the chile flakes, and cook 1 minute. Stir in the chopped
carrots, and cook 1 minute. Add 2 cups water, the red wine vinegar, lemon
juice, sugar, and salt, and bring to a boil. Cook, stirring occasionally, for
2 minutes.

2 Process the carrot mixture in a blender until smooth. If desired, pour the
sauce through a wire-mesh strainer into a bowl, discarding the solids.
Keep the sauce for up to a week in the refrigerator.

EXTRA CREDIT!

Serve with smoked salmon and
cream cheese, or pastrami and
poached eggs with Hollandaise.

3

Latkes are pancakes that are usually made with shredded potatoes. Carrot latkes, while not quite as crispy, are an amazing and inexpensive alternative. While this rendition may break with Jewish tradition, it allows you to cut some carbs without sacrificing flavor.

CARROT-GINGER LATKES

HANDS-ON: 10 MINUTES   TOTAL TIME: 20 MINUTES   SERVES 15

1 Stir together the shredded carrots, flour, scallions, parsley, ginger paste, garlic paste, 1 teaspoon salt, pepper, baking powder, and egg in a large bowl.

2 Heat 2 teaspoons of the oil a large nonstick skillet over medium-high. Working in batches and using a 2-inch cookie scoop, drop the carrot mixture into the hot oil in the skillet; press lightly to flatten the scoops into approximately 3-inch rounds. Cook until golden brown, about 3 minutes per side. Drain on paper towels, and season with the salt. Repeat the procedure with the remaining oil and carrot mixture. Serve hot.

10 medium carrots, steamed and shocked (page 65), shredded (about 3 cups)

½ cup all-purpose flour

½ cup finely chopped scallions

1 tablespoon chopped fresh flat-leaf parsley

1 teaspoon refrigerated ginger paste (from tube)

1 teaspoon refrigerated garlic paste (from tube)

1 teaspoon kosher salt, plus more for seasoning

1 teaspoon black pepper

½ teaspoon baking powder

1 large egg, beaten

2 tablespoons canola oil

4

1 tablespoon brined capers, drained

1 ½ tablespoons red wine vinegar

2 teaspoons refrigerated garlic paste (from tube)

2 teaspoons Dijon mustard

1 cup plus 2 tablespoons extra-virgin olive oil

½ cup roughly chopped fresh flat-leaf parsley

½ cup roughly chopped fresh basil

½ cup roughly chopped fresh mint

3 tablespoons fresh lemon juice

1 teaspoon kosher salt

1 teaspoon black pepper, plus more for seasoning

2 dashes of hot sauce, such as Tabasco

10 medium carrots, steamed and shocked (page 65), left whole

Crumbled feta cheese, for serving

Chopped fresh cilantro, for serving

EXTRA CREDIT!

Double the dressing recipe, and use the extra to marinate chicken, drizzle over seared steak, or pump up any salad.

I found myself dressing everything but myself in this herb dressing at Market & Rye. It's a go-to topping during the winter with our vegetarian Eggs Benedict, and I have more recently learned how awesome it is with charred carrots and feta cheese—if you've never tried rich, tangy feta, trust me, this is definitely the time to give it a spin!

CHARRED CARROT SALAD WITH HERB DRESSING AND FETA

HANDS-ON: 10 MINUTES   TOTAL TIME: 20 MINUTES   SERVES 4

1 Pulse the capers, red wine vinegar, garlic paste, and mustard in a food processor until the capers are finely chopped. Add 1 cup of the oil, the parsley, basil, mint, lemon juice, salt, 1 teaspoon pepper, and hot sauce, and process until smooth.

2 Preheat a grill pan or broiler to high. Toss the carrots in the remaining 2 tablespoons oil. Add the carrots to the hot grill pan and cook until charred and blackened, or broil them on a foil-lined baking sheet until blackened and slightly blistered, about 8 to 10 minutes. Toss the carrots with the desired amount of the herb dressing. Top with the feta and cilantro, and season with additional pepper to taste.

I knew I had to have this carrot-zucchini muffin in the book, but when I went in my pantry to reach for baking soda I saw cranberries and a lightbulb went off! Just adding one ingredient that is out of the norm really elevates these muffins and distracts the kids from the duo of veggies that I've slipped into these.

CARROT, CRANBERRY, AND ZUCCHINI MUFFINS

HANDS-ON: 10 MINUTES   TOTAL TIME: 40 MINUTES   MAKES 16

1 Preheat the oven to 375°F. Place 16 paper baking cups in the muffin pans.

2 Whisk together the sugar, flour, cinnamon, baking powder, baking soda, and salt in a large bowl. Fold in the shredded carrots and zucchini.

3 Whisk together the oil, egg, and vanilla until blended; add to the carrot mixture, and stir until combined. (It may not seem like a lot of liquid, but keep mixing because the oil will bind everything together.) Fold in the cranberries. Spoon about ¼ cup of the batter into each paper muffin cup.

4 Bake until a toothpick inserted into the center of a muffin comes out clean, 20 to 25 minutes. Cool in the pans on a wire rack for 5 minutes; remove the muffins from the pans, and cool completely on the rack.

1 ½ cups sugar

1 ½ cups all-purpose flour

1 teaspoon ground cinnamon

¾ teaspoon baking powder

¾ teaspoon baking soda

½ teaspoon kosher salt

10 medium carrots, steamed and shocked (page 65), shredded (about 3 cups)

1 cup shredded zucchini

¾ cup vegetable oil

1 large egg, beaten

1 teaspoon vanilla extract

1 cup sweetened dried cranberries

KALE

You might not have given kale a chance because you're used to seeing it on a sad breakfast diner plate as a wilty garnish alongside an orange slice, but it's time to tap into its wonderful potential. From raw to baked to stewed and beyond, my spins on this super-healthy green will become your new favorites. Prep your kale in advance to save time during the week. Wash the kale and pat dry with a paper towel. Refrigerate the washed and dried kale wrapped in a paper towel for 3 to 5 days. To remove the stem, strip the leaves off with your hands. You're now ready to jump into these easy dishes.

RAW KALE

For a bitter green, lacinato kale (also sold as dinosaur kale) has the sweetest finish. It also has the best texture of any type of kale, both when it's raw and after it's cooked. If you can't find lacinato, go ahead and try these recipes with a different variety of kale—they'll still be tasty.

START WITH: LACINATO KALE

1 KALE CAESAR
2 KALE SALSA VERDE
3 KALE SOUP
4 KALE "COLLARDS"
5 TURKEY "KALESSEROLE"

If you're a Caesar fan but hate anchovies, this salad can be your new fix. Finally, a killer Caesar salad that's not doused in anchovy flavor. My dressing is a great alternative that still packs a punch. If you want to get super technical, Worcestershire sauce actually has anchovies in it. To make this 100 percent vegetarian, leave it out, and you'll still have a great dressing.

KALE CAESAR

HANDS-ON: 10 MINUTES **TOTAL TIME:** 10 MINUTES **SERVES** 2 TO 4

1 Pulse the croutons in a food processor until the mixture resembles coarse meal, 6 to 8 times. Set aside.

2 Process the mayonnaise, oil, lemon juice, capers, garlic paste, mustard, Worcestershire sauce, pepper, salt, and hot sauce in a food processor until smooth.

3 Coat the inside of a large mixing bowl with the dressing, and add the kale, Parmesan, and crushed croutons. Toss to coat. Add a pinch of the salt and pepper and, if desired, more of the cheese. Divide the salad among bowls, or present it family style. Serve immediately.

½ cup store-bought croutons

¼ cup mayonnaise

¼ cup vegetable oil

2 tablespoons fresh lemon juice

1 tablespoon brined capers, drained

1 tablespoon refrigerated garlic paste (from tube)

1 tablespoon Dijon mustard

2 teaspoons Worcestershire sauce

½ teaspoon black pepper, plus more as needed

¼ teaspoon kosher salt, plus more as needed

3 dashes of hot sauce, such as Tabasco

6 cups thin strips lacinato kale leaves, stems discarded

½ cup freshly grated Parmesan cheese (2 ounces), plus more if desired

2

Mexican salsa verde (green sauce) is typically made with tomatillos, but my California remix swaps them for kale, creating a tangy go-to dressing for shrimp, fish, pork chops, pasta, or even peaches. If you don't like buttery and creamy sauces, this will be your friend. Of course, you can just eat it with tortilla chips.

KALE SALSA VERDE

HANDS-ON: 10 MINUTES   **TOTAL TIME: 10 MINUTES**   **SERVES 4 TO 6**

1 cup finely chopped lacinato kale leaves, stems discarded

¾ cup extra-virgin olive oil

½ cup loosely packed roughly chopped fresh flat-leaf parsley

¼ cup fresh lemon juice

¼ cup loosely packed roughly chopped fresh mint leaves

¼ cup roughly chopped fresh chives

2 tablespoons refrigerated garlic paste (from tube)

2 tablespoons brined capers, drained

1 tablespoon red wine vinegar

1 ½ teaspoons kosher salt

1 teaspoon black pepper

Pulse all the ingredients in a food processor until smooth, 8 to 10 times. Take care not to overmix and heat up the blade, as that would oxidize the herbs and change the taste. Refrigerate in an airtight container for 3 to 5 days.

EXTRA CREDIT!

Can you take the heat?
Add a fresh jalapeño.

Kale doesn't have to be super virtuous all the time. In fact, it just loves being paired with some good old fatty bacon. People will think you toiled over this soup for hours, but it's actually something you can do in far less time.

KALE SOUP

HANDS-ON: 10 MINUTES   TOTAL TIME: 35 MINUTES   SERVES 6 TO 8

1 Cook the bacon in a stockpot over medium-high, stirring occasionally, until browned, about 5 minutes. Add the turkey, salt, black pepper, onion powder, garlic salt, and chile flakes, and cook, using a spoon to break up the turkey, until the turkey is cooked through, 5 to 7 minutes. Drain through a fine wire-mesh strainer into a bowl; return the solids to the stockpot, discarding the fat in the bowl. Add the oil, onion, carrots, garlic paste, and hot sauce to the stockpot, and cook, stirring often, for 10 minutes. Pour through the strainer again; return the solids to the stockpot, and discard the fat in the bowl.

2 Stir the chicken stock, beans, and 2 cups water into the stockpot. Bring to a boil, and then remove from the heat. Add the kale leaves, and let stand, covered with the lid, until the kale is tender, 5 to 10 minutes. Stir when ready to serve, and garnish each serving with the grated Parmesan cheese.

6 slices bacon, chopped

1 pound ground turkey

1 teaspoon kosher salt

1 teaspoon black pepper

1 teaspoon onion powder

1 teaspoon garlic salt

½ teaspoon red chile flakes

2 tablespoons vegetable oil

2 cups chopped red onion

1 cup chopped carrots

1 tablespoon refrigerated garlic paste (from tube)

3 dashes of hot sauce, such as Tabasco

4 cups chicken stock

1 (15-ounce) can cannellini beans, drained and rinsed

2 cups water

3 cups loosely packed ½-inch-pieces lacinato kale leaves, stems discarded

Freshly grated Parmesan cheese, for garnish

EXTRA CREDIT!

Kick it up a notch with a squeeze of lemon and a few hits of Tabasco.

Can I be honest? I've never really liked collard greens—they look like wet towels in a bucket to me. I think it's a texture issue, so swapping in kale makes for a much better dish in my opinion. It's extra garlicky as a tribute to Gilroy, the garlic capital of California, near where I grew up, but the use of balsamic vinegar gives it a touch of sweet.

KALE "COLLARDS"

HANDS-ON: 10 MINUTES   TOTAL TIME: 25 MINUTES   SERVES 4 TO 5

1 Cook the bacon in a large skillet or Dutch oven over medium-high, stirring occasionally, until crispy, about 5 minutes. Add the onion, garlic paste, and chili paste, and cook, stirring occasionally, until the onions are tender, 5 to 7 minutes. Add the kale, and cook, stirring constantly, until it's completely broken down, 2 to 3 minutes. Add the chicken stock and salt, and bring to a boil. Cover and reduce the heat to medium-low; simmer for 10 minutes.

2 Remove the lid; stir in the balsamic vinegar, and simmer, uncovered, for 5 minutes. Remove from the heat, and put the lid back on until ready to serve.

4 slices bacon, diced

1 cup diced red onion

1 tablespoon refrigerated garlic paste (from tube)

1 tablespoon refrigerated chili paste (from tube)

12 cups packed 1-inch-wide strips lacinato kale leaves and stems

2 cups chicken stock

½ teaspoon kosher salt

2 tablespoons balsamic vinegar

5

3 tablespoons vegetable oil

1 pound ground turkey

2 cups chopped yellow onion

1 tablespoon refrigerated garlic paste (from tube)

1 teaspoon kosher salt

1 teaspoon black pepper

8 cups chopped lacinato kale leaves, stems discarded

1 (15.5-ounce) can chickpeas, drained and rinsed

2 cups cooked quinoa

¼ teaspoon crushed red pepper

1 cup sour cream

2 cups shredded Cheddar cheese (8 ounces)

½ cup plain fine, dried breadcrumbs

Why make a boring old casserole when you can whip up a creative new "Kalesserole"? I like using ground turkey here to keep this on the light side, but you can easily swap it for ground beef or pork if that's what you have on hand or prefer.

TURKEY "KALESSEROLE"

HANDS-ON: 25 MINUTES   TOTAL TIME: 45 MINUTES   SERVES 6 TO 8

1 Preheat the oven to 400°F. Coat a 2- to 3-quart oval or rectangular baking dish with cooking spray.

2 Heat 2 tablespoons of the oil in a large skillet over medium-high. Add the turkey and onion, and cook until slightly browned, about 10 minutes. Add the garlic paste, salt, and pepper; cook until fragrant, about 2 more minutes. Transfer the mixture to a large bowl.

3 Add the kale and the remaining 1 tablespoon oil to the skillet. Cook over medium-high until the kale is tender but still has a slight crunch, 3 to 5 minutes. Remove from the heat.

4 Add the cooked kale to the turkey mixture. Stir in the chickpeas, quinoa, and crushed red pepper. Add the sour cream and 1 ½ cups of the cheese, and stir until thoroughly incorporated. Transfer the mixture to the prepared baking dish. Top with the breadcrumbs.

5 Bake until the breadcrumbs are golden brown, about 15 minutes. Top with the remaining ½ cup cheese, and bake until the cheese melts, about 5 more minutes.

Want an even lighter dish? Substitute fat-free Greek yogurt for the sour cream.

PORTOBELLO MUSHROOMS

The portobello mushroom is no mere stand-in for meat—it's a juicy replacement that truly stands out on its own. It has kind of a bad rap from its overuse in the eighties, but it definitely deserves to remain in the limelight. A tight vehicle for flavor, the portobello can be cooked in so many different ways and really clings to any ingredients that you use with it. Marinate and roast some portobellos in my fine brine, and you'll be on your way to creating a palette of sensational 'shroom dishes.

START WITH: MARINATED-AND-ROASTED PORTOBELLOS

1 BELLO GHANOUSH
2 PORTOBELLO SALSA
3 PORTOBELLO-OLIVE MAYO
4 PORTOBELLO RANCH FRIES
5 MOZZARELLA-STUFFED CRISPY PORTOBELLO BURGERS

After I competed on the show *Top Chef,* I did a lot of cooking competitions with mystery-basket challenges. One particularly fun one was at the Gilroy Garlic Festival in California. Portobellos were the main ingredient, and I immediately thought of this all-purpose marinade—one of my secret weapons—that helped me win the challenge. The mushrooms get more delicious the longer they sit in the marinade, so don't be afraid to take your time with this. Make an extra batch of these mushrooms to use for several meals.

MARINATED-AND-ROASTED PORTOBELLOS

**HANDS-ON: 10 MINUTES   TOTAL TIME: 1 HOUR 30 MINUTES
MAKES 6**

1 Whisk together the onion, olive oil, wine, red wine vinegar, soy sauce, balsamic vinegar, lemon juice, and garlic paste in a 13- x 9-inch baking dish or roasting pan. Add the mushrooms to the marinade, turning them to coat both sides. Cover and chill for 1 to 3 hours.

2 Preheat the oven to 400°F. Put the mushroom caps, gill sides up, on an aluminum foil-lined baking sheet, and bake until tender, about 20 minutes. Sprinkle with the salt and pepper.

Don't rinse the mushrooms to clean them. Use a damp paper towel to brush off the dirt.

¼ cup minced red onion

¾ cup olive oil

¼ cup dry white wine

3 tablespoons red wine vinegar

3 tablespoons soy sauce

2 tablespoons balsamic vinegar

2 tablespoons fresh lemon juice

½ tablespoon refrigerated garlic paste (from tube)

6 portobello mushrooms, cleaned, stems removed

½ teaspoon kosher salt

½ teaspoon black pepper

EXTRA CREDIT!

Combine the remaining marinade (about 1 cup) with 2 tablespoons Dijon mustard, ¼ teaspoon kosher salt, and ¼ teaspoon black pepper. Pulse in a blender for a creamy vinaigrette. Makes 1¼ cups.

Don't judge a book by its color: Portobellos have kind of a drab hue, but take a chance on a first date with this rich veggie dish, and you'll keep coming back for its intense wow factor! Use this as a party dip or as a base sauce for fish, shrimp, chicken, or pasta dishes.

BELLO GHANOUSH

HANDS-ON: 10 MINUTES   **TOTAL TIME:** 20 MINUTES   **SERVES 6**

¾ cup olive oil

1 large eggplant, diced (about 5 cups)

1 medium-sized yellow onion, diced

½ tablespoon kosher salt

2 tablespoons refrigerated garlic paste (from tube)

½ teaspoon red chile flakes

2 Marinated-and-Roasted Portobellos (page 89), chopped

¼ cup tahini (sesame paste)

¼ cup fresh lemon juice

2 dashes of hot sauce, such as Tabasco

1 cup very cold water, plus more if needed

2 tablespoons chopped fresh mint leaves

1 tablespoon toasted sesame seeds

1 Heat the oil in a large saucepan over medium. Add the eggplant, onion, and salt, and cook, stirring often, until caramelized and tender, about 10 minutes. Add the garlic paste and chile flakes, and cook 1 more minute.

2 Transfer the eggplant mixture to the bowl of a food processor, and add the chopped mushrooms, tahini, lemon juice, and hot sauce. Process until finely chopped. With the food processor running, drizzle in the very cold water, and process until smooth, adding more water if necessary. Serve hot or cold, topped with the mint and toasted sesame seeds. Store in the refrigerator for up to 1 day, covered tightly with plastic wrap.

EXTRA CREDIT!

Add cream cheese and fresh herbs like parsley or chives to the food processor for an even heartier party dip, or elevate it by serving it with crumbled feta or goat cheese on top.

When it comes to salsa, we usually think Mexican or Hawaiian, but why can't our definition be broader? Dip into this flavor-packed mushroom version with tortilla or vegetable chips, or serve it as a dressing for pork chops, pork loin, or fish.

PORTOBELLO SALSA

HANDS-ON: 10 MINUTES   TOTAL TIME: 15 MINUTES   SERVES 5

½ cup diced red onion

3 tablespoons fresh lemon juice

2 Marinated-and-Roasted Portobellos (page 89), diced

1 cup cherry tomato halves

1 fresh jalapeño chile, seeds removed, minced

¼ cup loosely packed fresh flat-leaf parsley leaves, chopped

1 teaspoon kosher salt

Combine the red onion and lemon juice in a medium bowl; let sit for 5 minutes. Stir in the diced mushrooms, the tomatoes, jalapeño, parsley, and salt. Serve immediately, or refrigerate in an airtight container for up to 5 days; the longer it sits, the better it gets.

Don't like parsley? Swap with mint, basil, or cilantro instead.

I once tried an olive mayonnaise as a French fry dip at a restaurant during my travels on the East Coast. I wanted to try to recreate it, but once I started to experiment, I think I topped the original! The salty-sweet marinade for the mushrooms goes really well with the brininess of the olives.

PORTOBELLO-OLIVE MAYO

HANDS-ON: 10 MINUTES   TOTAL TIME: 10 MINUTES   MAKES 3 CUPS

Process the chopped mushrooms and the olives in a food processor until smooth. Add the mayonnaise, lemon juice, garlic paste, and salt, and process until combined. Refrigerate in an airtight container for up to 3 days.

You can use canned olives instead of fresh ones if you don't mind sacrificing some of the briny flavor, but please don't add the liquid.

2 Marinated-and-Roasted Portobellos (page 89), roughly chopped

¼ cup Niçoise olives, pitted

1 cup mayonnaise

2 tablespoons fresh lemon juice

1 teaspoon refrigerated garlic paste (from tube)

½ teaspoon kosher salt

Who doesn't love French fries? An abbreviated, cheese-free, snack version of my portobello burger, this is the winky-winky, sneaky-sneaky way to get kids (and adults) to leave potatoes behind for mushrooms. Think outside the tater! But be careful, because you'll want to eat half of them before you even get a chance to serve them.

PORTOBELLO RANCH FRIES

HANDS-ON: 10 MINUTES   TOTAL TIME: 15 MINUTES   SERVES 4

1 Stir together the flour and ranch dressing mix in a shallow dish. Put the eggs in a second shallow dish, and the panko in a third shallow dish. Working with a few mushroom strips at a time, dredge them in the flour mixture, and then dip them in the eggs, shaking off the excess. Dredge the mushrooms in the panko (be sure the mushrooms are thoroughly coated).

2 Heat ½ inch of the oil in a medium skillet until the oil is sputtering. (If a few panko crumbs dropped in the oil turn golden quickly, you're ready to fry.) Fry the mushrooms, flipping frequently, until golden, 2 to 3 minutes. Transfer them to a plate lined with paper towels, and sprinkle with the salt and pepper. Serve with the flavored mayo.

1 cup all-purpose flour

1 tablespoon ranch dressing mix, such as Hidden Valley

3 large eggs, beaten

1 ½ cups panko (Japanese-style breadcrumbs)

4 Marinated-and-Roasted Portobellos (page 89), cut into 1-inch-wide strips

Canola oil, for frying

½ teaspoon kosher salt

¼ teaspoon black pepper

Portobello-Olive Mayo (page **93**), for serving

5

2 Marinated-and-Roasted Portobellos (page 89)

½ cup shredded mozzarella cheese (2 ounces)

¾ cup all-purpose flour

1 tablespoon ranch dressing mix, such as Hidden Valley

2 large eggs, beaten

1 cup panko (Japanese-style breadcrumbs)

Canola oil, for frying

¾ teaspoon kosher salt

⅜ teaspoon black pepper

2 hamburger buns of your choice

¼ cup Thousand Island Dressing (page 200)

¼ cup dill pickle chips

1 cup shredded iceberg lettuce

1 medium tomato, cut into 4 (¼-inch-thick) slices

There is a little restaurant you might've heard of in Manhattan—now with outposts everywhere—called Shake Shack. This sandwich is inspired by one of my favorite burgers they serve, which isn't a burger at all, but a vegetarian play featuring portobellos.

MOZZARELLA-STUFFED CRISPY PORTOBELLO BURGERS

HANDS-ON: 15 MINUTES   **TOTAL TIME:** 25 MINUTES   **SERVES 2**

1 Cut a slit in a thick side of each mushroom cap to form a pocket. (Do not cut them in half.) Carefully stuff ¼ cup of the mozzarella into each mushroom pocket with your fingers or a spoon, pressing and flattening the cheese as you stuff. (Do not overstuff; see Note.)

2 Stir together the flour and ranch dressing mix in a small bowl. Put the eggs in a second bowl and the panko in a third bowl. Dip both sides of each mushroom in the flour mixture; then dip in the eggs, and then dredge in the panko. (Make sure the mushrooms are thoroughly coated in the panko.)

3 Preheat the oven to 375°F. Heat ½ inch of the oil in a medium saucepan over medium until sputtering. (If a few panko crumbs dropped in the oil turn golden quickly, you're ready to fry.) Fry the mushrooms, flipping them frequently and keeping a close eye on them, until they turn golden and the cheese starts to melt, 4 to 5 minutes. Transfer to an aluminum foil–lined baking sheet, and bake until the cheese is fully melted, about 5 minutes. Transfer to a paper towel–lined plate, and season with ½ teaspoon of the salt and ¼ teaspoon of the pepper.

4 Slather the top and bottom halves of each bun with 1 tablespoon Thousand Island Dressing. Layer each bottom half with the pickles, lettuce, and 2 tomato slices. Sprinkle with the remaining ¼ teaspoon salt and ⅛ teaspoon pepper. Top with the fried mushrooms and the bun top.

This can be messy. Chill the burgers for 30 minutes after stuffing them with mozzarella to let them set up if you prefer a neater burger.

EXTRA CREDIT!
Bake the stuffed mushrooms on a foil-lined baking sheet in a preheated 375°F oven for 15 minutes for a healthier alternative to frying.

CHICKEN

There's no shame in purchasing a rotisserie chicken instead of roasting your own. Once you see how fast you can make a wide variety of recipes without sacrificing flavor, you may never roast a chicken yourself again!

I always recommend free-range rotisserie chicken if you can find one. Feel free to use whatever kind and brand of prepared chicken you like; just make sure that it is juicy and well-seasoned. To shred the rotisserie chicken, cut off the leg and breast meat and remove the bones. Then pull the meat apart.

START WITH: A ROTISSERIE CHICKEN

1 LESLEY'S BISCUIT CHICKEN TURNOVERS
2 CALIFORNIA CHINESE CHICKEN SALAD
3 COOL RANCH CHICKEN SALAD SANDWICHES
4 CHICKEN-AND-CORNBREAD TAMALE PIE
5 CHICKEN AND BUTTERNUT SQUASH ENCHILADAS
   WITH RED SAUCE

I named these turnovers after a dish my wife, Lesley, likes to make when she's looking for an extra-comforting meal. These turnovers make great school lunches and also freeze very well.

LESLEY'S BISCUIT CHICKEN TURNOVERS

HANDS-ON: 10 MINUTES   TOTAL TIME: 58 MINUTES   MAKES 16

1 Cook the onion, mushrooms, zucchini, 1 tablespoon of the thyme, oil, salt, garlic paste, and ½ teaspoon of the pepper in a medium skillet over medium-high, stirring often, until the vegetables are caramelized and the liquid has evaporated, about 10 minutes. Remove from the heat, and stir in the cream of mushroom soup, lemon juice, vinegar, and chicken. Let cool for 30 minutes.

2 Preheat the oven to 400°F. Line a rimmed baking sheet with aluminum foil and lightly coat it with cooking spray; set aside. Using a rolling pin or the empty soup can, roll out each biscuit into a 5-inch round. Brush the beaten egg on half of the each biscuit round, and top with 1 ½ tablespoons of the room-temperature chicken mixture. Fold each biscuit in half to enclose the filling, and press the edges to seal. Dip a fork in the flour, and press along the edges of each turnover to crimp them.

3 Coat the turnovers lightly with cooking spray, and sprinkle them with the remaining 2 teaspoons pepper (about ⅛ teaspoon pepper per turnover) and 1 ½ teaspoons thyme. Arrange them on the prepared baking sheet, making sure the turnovers don't touch each other. Bake until golden brown, 18 to 20 minutes.

Use the same method to make turnovers with ground beef or pork.

2 cups diced yellow onion

2 cups cremini mushrooms, quartered

1 cup chopped zucchini (skins on)

1 ½ tablespoons chopped fresh thyme leaves

2 teaspoons vegetable oil

1 ½ teaspoons kosher salt

1 teaspoon refrigerated garlic paste (from tube)

2 ½ teaspoons black pepper

1 (10.5-ounce) can condensed cream of mushroom soup

1 tablespoon fresh lemon juice

2 teaspoons red wine vinegar

2 cups shredded rotisserie chicken

Nonstick cooking spray

16 Pillsbury Grands! Frozen Buttermilk Biscuits, thawed or 2 (16.3 ounce) cans refrigerated buttermilk biscuits

1 large egg, beaten

All-purpose flour, for crimping edges

Chinese chicken salad has been on the menu of every place I've ever worked, whether in a fancy version or a funky concoction. My Golden State take on the classic trades iceberg lettuce for cabbage and raw vegetables. It's clean, light, and incredibly simple.

CALIFORNIA CHINESE CHICKEN SALAD

HANDS-ON: 15 MINUTES   TOTAL TIME: 30 MINUTES   SERVES 6

SOY SESAME DRESSING (makes 2 cups)

½ cup soy sauce

½ cup rice wine vinegar

2 tablespoons tahini (sesame paste)

1 tablespoon honey

1 tablespoon refrigerated garlic paste
(from tube)

1 large pasteurized egg yolk

1 jalapeño chile, seeds removed, diced

¾ cup vegetable oil

1 teaspoon kosher salt

1 teaspoon black pepper

SALAD

1 (3-ounce) package instant Asian
noodle (ramen) soup mix

2 cups shredded rotisserie chicken

2 cups shredded napa cabbage

1 cup thinly sliced red onion

1 cup diced fresh mango

1 cup peeled and shredded jicama

¾ cup sliced cucumber, seeded

¾ cup shredded carrots

½ cup salted peanuts, chopped

½ cup loosely packed fresh cilantro
leaves, chopped

½ cup sliced scallions

½ cup toasted sesame seeds

2 tablespoons fresh lemon juice

1 Prepare the dressing: Process the soy sauce, vinegar, tahini, honey, garlic paste, egg yolk, and jalapeño in a blender until smooth. With the blender running, pour the oil through the opening in the lid in a slow, steady stream, processing until smooth. Sprinkle with ½ teaspoon each of salt and black pepper.

2 Prepare the salad: Crush the ramen noodles. (Reserve the flavor packet for another use.) Toss together the chicken, cabbage, red onion, mango, jicama, cucumber, carrots, peanuts, cilantro, scallions, sesame seeds, crushed ramen noodles, and the remaining ½ teaspoon each salt and black pepper in a large bowl. Drizzle with the lemon juice; add ¾ cup of the dressing, and toss to thoroughly coat. (Use any leftover dressing as a marinade for chicken, pork, steak, or shrimp.)

Not into using raw egg? Substitute 1 tablespoon of Dijon mustard.

EXTRA CREDIT!

Add fresh or canned mandarin orange segments for a bright boost of citrus.

Why serve chips on the side of a sandwich when they can be the star of the sandwich itself? A sneaky crunch from an unexpected place made this sandwich an early hit at my restaurant Market & Rye.

COOL RANCH CHICKEN SALAD SANDWICHES

HANDS-ON: 5 MINUTES   **TOTAL TIME: 5 MINUTES**   **SERVES 2**

1 Stir together the chicken, mayonnaise, ranch dressing mix, and lemon juice in a bowl.

2 Put 2 cheese slices on each of 2 bread slices, and microwave, 1 bread slice at a time, on High until the cheese is melted, about 20 seconds. Put 1 or 2 avocado slices and 2 lettuce leaves on each of the remaining 2 bread slices. Top each with about 1 cup of the chicken salad, and crown them with a handful of the Doritos. Put a cheesy bread slice on top to complete the sandwiches, and serve immediately. (Cover and store any leftover chicken salad for up to 1 day in the refrigerator.)

2 cups shredded rotisserie chicken, both white and dark meat

¼ cup mayonnaise

1 tablespoon ranch dressing mix, such as Hidden Valley

1 tablespoon fresh lemon juice

4 slices pepper Jack cheese

4 slices white bread, toasted

1 ripe avocado, pitted, peeled, and sliced

4 iceberg lettuce leaves

1 (11-ounce) package Cool Ranch Doritos

4

2 tablespoons vegetable oil

1 cup diced red bell pepper

1 cup diced green bell pepper

1 cup diced yellow onion

1 jalapeño chile, seeds removed, diced

1 ½ tablespoons refrigerated garlic paste (from tube)

1 ½ teaspoons kosher salt

1 teaspoon chili powder

1 teaspoon ground cumin

1 ½ tablespoons, plus 1 teaspoon taco seasoning

3 cups shredded rotisserie chicken

1 (10.5-ounce) can cream of chicken soup

1 cup cherry tomatoes, halved

1 cup frozen sweet corn

1 (7-ounce) can diced green chiles

½ cup chunky salsa

½ cup sour cream

1 cup loosely packed chopped fresh cilantro leaves

1 (7.5-ounce) package yellow corn muffin mix, such as Martha White

½ cup whole milk

Cornbread mix is another friend in the kitchen that can do so much more than just what's on the back of the box. Here, it's the basis for a truly memorable tamale pie. Warning: You might eat too much. ☺

CHICKEN-AND-CORNBREAD TAMALE PIE

HANDS-ON: 10 MINUTES   TOTAL TIME: 40 MINUTES   SERVES 8

1 Preheat the oven to 400°F. Heat the oil in a medium skillet over medium-high; add the red pepper, green pepper, onion, jalapeño, garlic paste, salt, chili powder, cumin, and 1 ½ tablespoons of the taco seasoning, and cook, stirring often, until the vegetables are softened, 8 to 10 minutes. Remove from the heat, and stir in the chicken, cream of chicken soup, tomatoes, corn, green chiles, salsa, sour cream, and ½ cup of the cilantro until the ingredients are evenly distributed.

2 Place a 9-inch square baking pan on an aluminum foil-lined rimmed baking sheet; pour the chicken mixture into the 9-inch pan, creating an even layer. Stir together the corn muffin mix, remaining 1 teaspoon taco seasoning, and remaining ½ cup cilantro in a medium bowl; add the milk, and stir until well blended. Spread the corn muffin batter evenly over the chicken mixture. Bake until golden brown on top, about 30 minutes.

I was raised on what I think of as "Americanized Mexican food," also known as chicken with salsa and sour cream! Nearly equal amounts of chicken and veggies make this flavorful dish very affordable, and the frozen squash is a big time-saver.

CHICKEN AND BUTTERNUT SQUASH ENCHILADAS WITH RED SAUCE

HANDS-ON: 15 MINUTES   TOTAL TIME: 35 MINUTES   SERVES 5

1 Preheat the oven to 400°F. Cook the onion, squash, oil, jalapeño, and garlic paste in a medium skillet over medium-high, stirring often, until the vegetables are tender, about 12 minutes. Remove from the heat, and stir in the chicken, green chiles, salsa, taco seasoning, salt, and 1 cup of the cheese.

2 Put the stack of tortillas on a microwave-safe plate, and cover them with a damp paper towel. Microwave on High until softened, about 1 minute. Keep the tortillas covered until ready to use.

3 Spread 1 cup of the enchilada sauce in the bottom of a 13- x 9-inch baking dish; pour the remaining sauce in a shallow bowl. Working with 1 tortilla at a time, dip the tortillas into the sauce in the bowl, and fill each with ½ cup of the chicken mixture. Roll up the tortillas like a cigar, and arrange them, seam sides down, in the baking dish, nestled next to each other. Cover the enchiladas with the sauce remaining in the bowl, and sprinkle them with the remaining 1 cup cheese.

4 Bake until the sauce is bubbly, about 15 minutes. Increase the heat to broil; broil until the cheese is brown and crispy on top, 2 to 4 minutes.

If you are using fresh salsa from the store, drain the liquid before adding to the enchiladas.

Substitute shredded mozzarella or sharp Cheddar cheese for the four-cheese blend, if you like.

2 ½ cups diced yellow onion

1 ½ cups frozen butternut squash cubes

3 tablespoons vegetable oil

1 jalapeño chile, seeds removed, diced

2 tablespoons refrigerated garlic paste (from tube)

2 cups shredded rotisserie chicken

1 (7-ounce) can chopped green chiles

1 cup chunky salsa (see Note)

1 ½ tablespoons mild taco seasoning

1 teaspoon kosher salt

2 cups shredded Mexican 4-cheese blend (about 8 ounces)

10 (6-inch) corn tortillas

1 (16-ounce) can red enchilada sauce, such as Las Palmas

BACON

Believe it or not, I was actually a vegetarian for years. But, like so many other people I know, bacon ended up becoming my gateway drug back into the world of meat. My Brown Sugar–Black Pepper Bacon is a showstopper on its own, but once you've made a batch, you've unlocked the path toward a pair of outrageously good breakfast meals, plus scones and cornbread that will be highlights of your baking arsenal, and a memorable marmalade that you'll want to serve with absolutely everything.

Throughout my travels on the East Coast, I would see candied bacon on menus so frequently that I was finally motivated to come up with my own. I love the way the herbal note of the rosemary works with the fat, juicy smokiness of the bacon, the kick of the black pepper, and the sweetness of the brown sugar. It tastes like Christmas, no matter the time of year—and that's a good thing.

3 tablespoons light brown sugar

1 tablespoon chopped fresh rosemary

1 tablespoon black pepper, preferably freshly ground

16 slices thick-cut bacon

BROWN SUGAR–BLACK PEPPER BACON

HANDS-ON: 5 MINUTES   TOTAL TIME: 40 MINUTES   SERVES 16

1 Preheat the oven to 400°F. Combine the brown sugar, rosemary, and black pepper in a small bowl.

2 Line two rimmed baking sheets with aluminum foil; place a lightly greased wire rack in each. Arrange 8 bacon slices in a single layer on each rack.

3 Bake for 25 minutes, rotating the pans and sprinkling the brown sugar mixture over the bacon halfway through. Continue to bake until the bacon is browned and crisp, 10 to 12 minutes.

Consider cooking extra batches of this bacon and freezing them for future efficiency.

1 ¼ cups all-purpose flour

1 tablespoon baking powder

2 ½ teaspoons sugar

4 tablespoons unsalted butter, melted

1 large egg

¼ cup buttermilk

1 cup milk

1 teaspoon vanilla extract

2 bananas, diced

8 slices Brown Sugar–Black Pepper Bacon (page 113), each broken into 3 pieces

This hunka hunka burnin' breakfast is my take on Elvis' favorite meal, minus the peanut butter. Like the King, they're unapologetically messy. You may think the pancakes themselves need more sugar, but with the brown sugar in the bacon and the banana in the batter, I think you'll get your sweet fix here. This batter also makes excellent waffles.

ELVIS PANCAKES

HANDS-ON: 10 MINUTES   TOTAL TIME: 25 MINUTES   MAKES 24

1 Stir together the flour, baking powder, and sugar in a mixing bowl. Stir together the melted butter and egg in another mixing bowl, and mix well. Slowly add the buttermilk, milk, and vanilla to the butter and egg. Add the flour mixture to the buttermilk mixture, and blend until everything is moist and lumpy. Let the batter rest for 5 minutes.

2 Pour ¼ cup of the batter for each pancake into a hot skillet or griddle coated with nonstick cooking spray, and spread lightly. Cook over medium heat until the pancake starts bubbling and the underside is light brown, about 2 minutes. Once a crust has started to set, add 3 pieces of the banana and 3 pieces of the bacon to each pancake. Flatten with a spatula, and cook for another 3 minutes. Turn the pancake and cook until golden brown, about 2 minutes. Remove the pancakes, and keep them warm in a 200°F oven until ready to serve. Serve with butter and maple syrup.

For best results, use your crispiest bacon when you start.

EXTRA CREDIT!

Make Elvis syrup! Melt ¼ cup peanut butter with ½ cup maple syrup in a saucepan.

2

A beautiful and savory marmalade, this is fantastic served hot, cold, or at room temperature. Try it as a topping for clam chowder, an accompaniment to fried chicken and waffles, or a foil for a cheese plate. I guarantee that you'll eat this quicker than you're worried about it lasting. But if you must know, it should keep in the refrigerator for a few weeks and it freezes well, too.

BACON MARMALADE

HANDS-ON: 10 MINUTES   TOTAL TIME: 1 HOUR   SERVES 6

2 tablespoons vegetable oil

2 cups chopped yellow onion

1 teaspoon refrigerated garlic paste (from tube)

2 cups fresh brewed coffee

½ cup bourbon

½ cup red wine vinegar

½ cup maple syrup

6 tablespoons packed light or dark brown sugar

12 slices Brown Sugar–Black Pepper Bacon (page 113), chopped

1 Heat the oil in a stockpot over medium-high; add the onion and garlic paste, and cook, stirring constantly, for 5 minutes.

2 Stir in the coffee, bourbon, vinegar, maple syrup, brown sugar, and bacon, and bring to a slow rolling boil. Cook, stirring occasionally, until the mixture is reduced by about two-thirds and becomes darker and richer but not tacky, about 40 minutes.

EXTRA CREDIT!

Instead of bacon strips, substitute this marmalade to create over-the-top BLTs or add a dollop on a burger. Yum! ☺

Cornbread is probably one of my guiltiest pleasures in the world. If this rendition seems like it contains a lot of sugar, it's because it does—I just love the sweet and salty interplay between the sugar and the Brown Sugar–Black Pepper Bacon! Serve this with breakfast instead of toast, or make it a meal with Ryan's Beefy Pork Chili (page 143) and Kale "Collards" (page 83).

SWEET CORNBREAD WITH BACON AND CHEDDAR

HANDS-ON: 15 MINUTES   TOTAL TIME: 50 MINUTES   SERVES 9

1 Preheat the oven to 375°F. Generously grease a 2-inch-deep, 9-inch square pan with the butter.

2 Meanwhile, stir together the flour, cornmeal, cheese, sugar, bacon, salt, baking soda, and pepper in a medium bowl.

3 Whisk together the buttermilk, oil, and eggs in a separate bowl. Fold the buttermilk mixture into the flour mixture, and transfer the batter to the prepared pan. Bake until a toothpick or fork comes out clean, about 35 minutes. Spread the butter over the top, and cut into 9 squares; serve with the honey.

Cut the cornbread into cubes before freezing for easy reheating.

Softened unsalted butter, for the pan

1 ¼ cups all-purpose flour

1 cup fine cornmeal

3 ounces Cheddar cheese, shredded (about ¾ cup)

⅔ cup granulated sugar

½ cup roughly chopped Brown Sugar–Black Pepper Bacon (page 113)

1 ½ teaspoons kosher salt

¾ teaspoon baking soda

½ teaspoon black pepper

1 ¼ cups buttermilk

¼ cup vegetable oil

2 large eggs

2 tablespoons unsalted butter

2 tablespoons honey

EXTRA CREDIT!

This dish makes a great filling for a sandwich the next day. Serve it with mayo, mustard, pickles, lettuce, tomato, and onion.

I came up with this dish because I don't have a lot of time in general, and my wife hates washing dishes as much as I do. When designing my line of pots and pans a few years ago, I wanted to create a skillet that could do everything; this all-in-one breakfast recipe is the perfect go-to dish. Not only is it easy to make and beautiful to serve straight from the pan, it minimizes the mess you'll have to clean up later.

LAZY (WO) MAN'S ONE-PAN BREAKFAST

HANDS-ON: 15 MINUTES   TOTAL TIME: 35 MINUTES   SERVES 6

About 2 tablespoons kosher salt, plus more to taste

8 ounces fingerling potatoes, cut in half lengthwise

2 tablespoons extra-virgin olive oil

½ cup finely chopped yellow onion

½ cup cherry tomatoes halves

½ cup chopped salami

½ cup chopped Brown Sugar–Black Pepper Bacon (page 113)

1 pinch of black pepper, plus more to taste

1 pinch of red chile flakes (optional)

6 large eggs

¼ cup loosely packed fresh flat-leaf parsley leaves, chopped

Toast or tortillas, for serving

1 Fill a 10-inch skillet with water; add the salt (use just enough so the water tastes like the ocean), and bring to a boil over medium-high. Add the potatoes, and cook until tender when pierced with a fork, 8 to 10 minutes. Drain. Wipe the skillet clean.

2 Heat the oil in the skillet over medium-high. Return the potatoes to the skillet, and cook until browned, 8 to 10 minutes. Stir in the onion, and cook, stirring occasionally, until they are slightly browned, about 4 minutes. Add the tomatoes, salami, and chopped Brown Sugar–Black Pepper Bacon, the pinch of black pepper, and I encourage you to add a small amount of chile flakes for that sweet heat. Then cook for 2 more minutes.

3 Reduce the heat to low, and make 6 nests out of the potato mixture. Break 1 egg into the center of each nest. Sprinkle the eggs with the desired amount of salt and pepper. Push the potato mixture around the eggs, and let cook until the eggs are set, about 2 minutes. (Don't stress if you break a yolk! Let the eggs start to set for about 2 minutes—if you can begin to move them and they're attaching to the potatoes, that's a good sign.)

4 Sprinkle the parsley over the top. Remove the skillet from the heat, cover with a lid, and let sit for 4 minutes. Before serving, carefully drain off some of the oil by tipping the pan to the side; blot the top of the dish with a paper towel. Serve family style, in the pan, with the toast or tortillas.

5

12 ounces (1 ½ cups) chilled unsalted butter, cut into small pieces

3 ½ cups all-purpose flour, plus more for dusting

1 ½ cups fine cornmeal

½ cup packed light brown sugar

1 tablespoon plus 1 teaspoon baking powder

2 teaspoons black pepper

1 teaspoon kosher salt

1 cup chopped Brown Sugar–Black Pepper Bacon (page 113)

1 teaspoon roughly chopped fresh rosemary

1 large egg

1 large egg yolk

½ cup heavy cream

¼ cup whole milk

¼ cup honey

Nonstick cooking spray

2 tablespoons melted butter, for brushing

A lot of people don't know I have a pastry background, and that my version of therapy is baking. A scone is a great intro to different baking methods. If you, like me, get invited to a lot of potlucks, house parties, and birthdays, trust me—bring these scones and you'll be signing autographs all day.

BLACK PEPPER–BACON AND HONEY SCONES

HANDS-ON: 15 MINUTES   TOTAL TIME: 45 MINUTES   MAKES 1 DOZEN

1 Freeze the diced butter until firm, 15 to 20 minutes.

2 Preheat the oven to 400°F. Line a baking sheet with aluminum foil, and lightly grease it with cooking spray.

3 Process the flour, cornmeal, brown sugar, baking powder, pepper, and salt in a food processor until well combined. Remove half of the flour mixture, and reserve it in a large bowl. Add the cold butter to the remaining flour mixture in the food processor, and pulse until large and small pebbles form. Add the butter mixture to the reserved flour mixture; combine them using your hand until just pebbly (do not overmix). Fold in the bacon and rosemary.

4 Whisk together the egg, egg yolk, cream, milk, and honey; slowly fold the egg mixture into the flour and butter mixture. Turn the mixture out onto a lightly floured surface; dust the top with flour. Press the mixture down, making sure to remove any air bubbles, and roughly shape it into an 8-inch round that's about 1 inch thick (make sure not to press too hard). Cut the dough into quarters; cut each quarter into three pizza-like wedges. Place the scones on the prepared baking sheet, and spray the scones with the cooking spray.

5 Bake until golden, 25 to 30 minutes, rotating the pan halfway through. Remove the scones from the pan to a wire rack, and brush them with the melted butter. Serve warm or at room temperature.

EXTRA CREDIT!

Never be afraid to add a tablespoon of bacon fat to the wet ingredients when you're mixing them in step 4. It will make the dish extra bacon-y. Nom, nom.

PORK

Ah, pork! As the famous National Pork Board slogan claims, it's the "other white meat," and it is much more of a chameleon than you might think. A 7-pound pork shoulder simmering all day in your slow-cooker on Sunday becomes the succulent foundation for quick-prep recipes throughout the week. For best consistency, use two forks to shred the pork roast.

Don't be intimidated by the size of the pork roast that you're working with; your slow cooker is magic and is going to do pretty much all of the work for you. Wake up in the morning, take a few minutes to brown the pork, and then set it and forget it—you'll be on your way to something pretty special.

MANY ONIONS PORK SHOULDER

HANDS-ON: 20 MINUTES   **TOTAL TIME:** 8 HOURS 20 MINUTES
MAKES 1 ROAST (ABOUT 8 CUPS SHREDDED MEAT)

1 tablespoon onion powder

1 tablespoon dried minced onion

1 teaspoon lemon pepper

1 teaspoon black pepper

1 teaspoon garlic salt

1 (7-pound) bone-in pork shoulder roast

2 tablespoons jarred chicken soup base, such as Better Than Bouillon

3 cups finely chopped yellow or white onion

1 (12-ounce) can beer

1 Stir together the onion powder, dried onion, lemon pepper, black pepper, and garlic salt in a small bowl; set aside.

2 Pat the pork dry with paper towels. Heat a large skillet over medium-high. Add the pork to the skillet, fat side down, and cook 10 to 12 minutes, turning to brown all sides. Transfer the pork to a 6-quart slow cooker, fat side up, and rub the chicken soup base all over it. Rub the spice mixture all over the pork, and then add the onion and beer to the pot. Cover and cook on low until tender, about 8 hours.

3 Transfer the pork from the slow cooker to a cutting board, and let it cool for 15 minutes before removing the bone and dividing the meat into large portions. Cool the cooking liquid about 15 minutes, and then skim the fat from the top. Refrigerate any leftovers in an airtight container, with some of the cooking liquid to keep it juicy; or you can also freeze portions of the pork up to 1 month.

Growing up in California, I was raised on tacos, but it wasn't until I traveled to Mexico that I really learned the different styles. Trying real street tacos in Zihuatanejo blew my mind and turned me on to the art of simplicity. This will likely become a meal that everyone asks you to make over and over.

SCOTT STREET TACOS (CARNITAS)

HANDS-ON: 20 MINUTES   TOTAL TIME: 20 MINUTES   SERVES 8

½ cup diced red onion

2 tablespoons finely chopped jalapeño chile

2 tablespoons fresh lemon juice

½ teaspoon kosher salt

¼ teaspoon black pepper

2 cups loosely packed finely shredded cabbage

½ cup chopped fresh cilantro

½ cup chopped scallions

2 tablespoons vegetable oil

2 cups shredded Many Onions Pork Shoulder (page 125)

¼ cup water

8 (6-inch) corn tortillas

1 large ripe avocado, pitted, peeled, and cut into 16 slices

Hot sauces, for serving

1 Soak the red onion in cold water for 5 minutes to mellow its flavor; drain. Stir together the red onion, jalapeño, lemon juice, salt, and pepper in a medium bowl, and let stand 5 minutes to allow the flavors to develop. Stir in the cabbage, cilantro, and scallions.

2 Heat the oil in a medium skillet over medium-high. Add the shredded pork, and cook until the meat is lightly browned and the edges are crisp, 2 to 3 minutes. Add ¼ cup water to the skillet, and cook until the moisture evaporates, 1 to 2 minutes, stirring to loosen any browned bits from the bottom of the skillet.

3 Char the tortillas over an open flame if you have a gas grill, or warm them in the oven. Place 2 slices of avocado on each tortilla, followed by about ¼ cup of the pork. Top each taco with the slaw mixture, and serve with a selection of hot sauces on the side.

To achieve the right texture for the slaw, the cabbage should be shredded as thinly as angel-hair pasta.

EXTRA CREDIT!

Serve with my Carrot Hot Sauce (page 68).

2

Here's a little shout-out to my culturally diverse San Francisco neighborhood. My wife and I are fond of a Vietnamese restaurant that serves a classic vermicelli-packed salad called *bun,* and this is my rendition of it. Don't be afraid of fish sauce; it's literally a game changer.

SAN FRANCISCO VIETNAMESE PORK SALAD

HANDS-ON: 20 MINUTES   TOTAL TIME: 20 MINUTES   SERVES 2

1 cup water

¼ cup sugar

¼ cup Asian fish sauce

¼ cup fresh lemon juice

2 tablespoons finely chopped jalapeño chile

2 teaspoons refrigerated garlic paste (from tube)

1 teaspoon Asian chili paste

2 cups cold, roughly chopped Many Onions Pork Shoulder (page 125)

4 cups roughly chopped red leaf lettuce

3 ounces rice vermicelli, soaked according to package directions and drained

1 cup thinly sliced English cucumber

⅔ cup shredded carrots

½ cup loosely packed fresh cilantro leaves

½ cup loosely packed fresh mint leaves

2 tablespoons sliced scallions

2 tablespoons roughly chopped roasted peanuts

1 lime

1 Preheat the broiler. Line a rimmed baking sheet with aluminum foil.

2 Bring 1 cup water and the sugar to a boil in a small saucepan over medium-high, stirring to dissolve the sugar. Remove from the heat, and stir in the fish sauce, lemon juice, jalapeño, garlic paste, and chili paste. Set aside.

3 Spread the chopped pork in an even layer on the prepared pan; pour ¼ cup of the fish sauce dressing over the pork.

4 Broil the pork 4 to 5 inches from the heat source until the meat is crunchy, about 6 minutes. Reserve the pan juices.

5 Divide the lettuce between two bowls, and top each with half of the vermicelli, half of the cucumber slices, and half of the carrots. Sprinkle with the cilantro and mint, and top each with half of the pork. Pour the juices from the baking sheet over the salads, and scatter the scallions and peanuts on top. Finish with a squeeze of lime, and serve with the remaining fish sauce dressing portioned into two small cups.

Lesley and I got married in Hawaii, and we used the hashtag #MauiMe to keep track of our social media memories. These tasty pork sliders served on sweet Hawaiian-style dinner rolls remind me of that wonderful time! Here, I've infused my slow-cooker pork with a hint of sweetness to approximate the taste of Hawaiian kalua pork, which is wrapped in a banana leaf and cooked in the ground for 24 hours.

#MAUIME SLIDERS

HANDS-ON: 15 MINUTES   TOTAL TIME: 40 MINUTES   SERVES 6

1 Whisk together the mayonnaise, lemon juice, sesame seeds, soy sauce, pepper, and ¼ teaspoon of the salt in a medium bowl. Add the cabbage, and gently stir to coat.

2 Heat the oil in a large skillet over medium. Add the onion and cook, covered with a lid, until softened, about 10 minutes, stirring halfway through. Remove the lid, increase the heat to medium-high, and add the shredded pork, chicken stock, and banana. Cover partially with the lid, and cook until the liquid is reduced to about ¼ cup, about 10 minutes. Remove and discard the banana. Add the remaining ¼ teaspoon salt, and cook until the liquid is reduced to about 2 tablespoons, about 2 minutes.

3 Divide the pork and slaw evenly among the toasted rolls.

¼ cup mayonnaise

2 tablespoons fresh lemon juice

1 tablespoon toasted sesame seeds

1 teaspoon soy sauce

¼ teaspoon black pepper

½ teaspoon kosher salt

3 cups firmly packed finely shredded cabbage

2 tablespoons vegetable oil

1 cup diced yellow onion

2 cups shredded Many Onions Pork Shoulder (page 125)

1 cup chicken stock

1 banana, peeled and left whole

1 (12-ounce) package Hawaiian sweet dinner rolls, split and toasted

4

Nonstick cooking spray

1 cup cold chopped Many Onions Pork Shoulder (page 125)

3 cups cold prepared macaroni and cheese

1 cup shredded mozzarella cheese (4 ounces)

⅓ cup chopped fresh chives, plus more for garnish

½ teaspoon kosher salt

½ teaspoon black pepper

⅓ cup instant-blending flour, such as Wondra

1 (16-ounce) package refrigerated egg roll wrappers

2 large eggs, beaten

Sriracha chili sauce, for serving

Mac and cheese egg rolls are a throwback from my old 3-Sum Eats food truck. This dish follows me like a 1990's arm-band tattoo, but I am proud of it. Adding pork to the recipe just takes it straight over the top—right where you wanna be.

BAKED PORK MAC AND CHEESE EGG ROLLS

**HANDS-ON: 15 MINUTES   TOTAL TIME: 30 MINUTES
SERVES 16 AS AN APPETIZER**

1 Preheat the oven to 475°F. Line a baking sheet with aluminum foil, and coat the foil with the nonstick cooking spray. Stir together the chopped pork, macaroni and cheese, mozzarella, chives, salt, and pepper in a medium bowl.

2 Put the flour in a shallow bowl. Working with 1 egg roll wrapper at a time, spread out the wrapper on a clean work surface. Dip a brush into the beaten eggs, and brush the egg roll wrapper, coating it evenly. Using a ¼-cup measure, scoop a portion of the pork mixture onto the bottom third of the wrapper, and shape the filling into a hot dog shape. Fold the left and right sides of the wrapper in and over the ends of the hot dog shape, tightening and pressing to lock in the filling. Now, roll up the egg roll like you would roll a burrito, folding the wrapper over as you pull back on the filling and tighten as you roll so you don't lose any of the filling. This method will seal the egg roll completely. Lightly brush some beaten egg all over the egg roll, roll it in the flour to coat, and transfer to the prepared baking sheet. Repeat with the remaining pork mixture and egg roll wrappers. Coat each egg roll with the cooking spray.

3 Bake until well browned and crisp, 15 to 20 minutes. Transfer the egg rolls to a platter, garnish with the chives, and serve with the Sriracha chili sauce.

They get crunchier as they cool, so patience is a virtue here!

I always thought pozole was a hearty soup you only ate to cure a hangover, but I was so happy to find out I was wrong! I discovered that something wonderful and nourishing happens when you combine hominy, pork, and tortilla chips. Because we're using the slow-cooked pork, this is another dish that typically takes hours to prepare that you'll speed through in no time.

CALIFORNIA POZOLE VERDE

HANDS-ON: 20 MINUTES   TOTAL TIME: 50 MINUTES   SERVES 8

1 Heat the oil in a Dutch oven or other heavy-bottomed pot over medium-high. Add the jalapeño, onion, cumin, oregano, and salt, and cook, stirring often, until the onions are tender, about 5 minutes. Add the chicken stock, tomatillos, and salsa verde, and bring to a boil. Reduce the heat to medium, and simmer, stirring occasionally, for 10 minutes. Remove from the heat, and stir in the cilantro.

2 Process the mixture with an immersion blender until smooth. (Or let the soup cool for 10 minutes, and then process in batches in a blender until smooth, and return to the pot.) Stir in the shredded pork and hominy, and return to a boil. Reduce the heat to medium-low, and simmer, stirring occasionally, until slightly thickened, about 10 more minutes.

3 Ladle the soup into the bowls. Top each serving with the avocado, cabbage, and radishes. Sprinkle with the paprika, and serve with broken tostada shells or tortilla chips and a lime wedge.

2 tablespoons vegetable oil

2 jalapeño chiles, seeds removed, diced

1 cup chopped yellow onion

2 teaspoons ground cumin

1 teaspoon dried oregano

½ teaspoon kosher salt

6 cups chicken stock

3 (11-ounce) cans whole tomatillos, drained

1 cup salsa verde, such as La Victoria

1 cup firmly packed roughly chopped fresh cilantro leaves (about 1 bunch)

2 cups shredded Many Onions Pork Shoulder (page 125)

2 (15.5-ounce) cans hominy, drained

2 ripe avocados, pitted, peeled, and diced

2 cups loosely packed finely shredded cabbage

1 cup thinly sliced radishes

Smoked paprika, for sprinkling

16 tostada shells, broken into large pieces, or tortilla chips

2 limes, quartered, for serving

GROUND BEEF

Growing up, Mama Pat was the David Copperfield of ground beef—she could come up with so many different acts for it that it seemed like magic! Affordable, satisfying, and super simple to cook, ground beef is a great ally in the kitchen.

While many of the recipes in this book can be made in minutes, Mama Pat's Meat Sauce requires slow-cooking in the Crock-Pot; I like to cook it for a minimum of 8 hours. Trust me, though, it's worth the extra time to make this sauce! Master it and you'll have the building block for some of the most crowd-pleasing family favorites you can make!

START WITH: MAMA PAT'S MEAT SAUCE

1 FORK-AND-KNIFE SLOPPY JOES
2 SPAGHETTI CARBONARA(ISH)
3 EZ COTTAGE LASAGNA
4 RYAN'S BEEFY PORK CHILI
5 ROGUE POT PIE

When I was a kid, my younger brother, Steven, and I would walk home from school every day—and a good mile away from home, we'd start smelling my mother's Bolognese sauce. This is an adaptation of my mom's recipe, which itself was an adaptation of her mom's recipe. It gets better the longer it cooks and is also a particularly good item to keep stocked in the freezer all year round.

My favorite part of this recipe is that it's made in a slow cooker, which is unusual for a Bolognese. Start the night before and cook it overnight, or start in the morning and go to work, come home, throw in some pasta, and call it a day. It's the definition of "set it and forget it," not to mention inexpensive to make.

MAMA PAT'S MEAT SAUCE

HANDS-ON: 15 MINUTES   TOTAL TIME: 8 HOURS 15 MINUTES
MAKES: 10 CUPS

2 pounds ground beef

2 cups chopped yellow onion

2 tablespoons refrigerated garlic paste (from tube)

1 (28-ounce) can diced tomatoes

1 (28-ounce) can tomato sauce

1 (6-ounce) can tomato paste

2 tablespoons light brown sugar

1 tablespoon dried oregano

2 teaspoons kosher salt

1 teaspoon dried thyme

1 teaspoon garlic salt

1 teaspoon paprika

½ teaspoon black pepper

4 bay leaves

1 cup water

Combine the ground beef, onion, and garlic paste in a Dutch oven or large skillet over medium-high, and cook, stirring until the meat is browned and crumbled and the onion is tender, 8 to 10 minutes. Drain off the excess fat, and transfer the meat and onion mixture to a 5- or 6-quart slow cooker. Add the diced tomatoes, tomato sauce, tomato paste, brown sugar, oregano, salt, thyme, garlic salt, paprika, black pepper, bay leaves, and 1 cup water, and stir to combine. Cover and cook on Low for 8 hours. Discard the bay leaves before serving. (Refrigerate the sauce up to 5 days or freeze it.)

Feel free to substitute ground pork or turkey for the beef, but be aware that you may need to add some additional salt to the recipe when you switch proteins.

1

Sloppy Joes were another childhood staple in our household, one of my mom's multifaceted ways of stretching ground beef. I've resurrected it from the 1988 time warp via a fun little rendition that includes corn chips, Cheddar cheese, and a bun—all eaten with a fork and a knife.

FORK-AND-KNIFE SLOPPY JOES

HANDS-ON: 25 MINUTES   TOTAL TIME: 25 MINUTES   SERVES 4

1 tablespoon refrigerated chili paste
(from tube)

1 tablespoon refrigerated garlic paste
(from tube)

**3 cups Mama Pat's Meat Sauce
(page 137)**

½ cup bottled chili sauce
(such as Heinz)

1 ½ tablespoons light brown sugar

1 tablespoon Worcestershire sauce

½ teaspoon black pepper

½ teaspoon hot sauce

4 kaiser rolls or sturdy sandwich rolls of
your choice, cut in half

8 slices Cheddar cheese, such as
Tillamook

2 cups corn chips, such as Fritos, lightly
crushed

1 Preheat broiler with oven rack 6 inches from the heat. Combine the chili paste and garlic paste in a large nonstick skillet, and cook over medium until the mixture begins to bubble, 1 to 2 minutes. Stir in the meat sauce, chili sauce, brown sugar, Worcestershire sauce, pepper, and hot sauce. Increase the heat to medium-high, and bring to a boil; reduce the heat to medium, and simmer, stirring often, until the mixture has thickened, about 12 minutes.

2 Place the bottom halves of the rolls, cut sides up, on a broiler pan; broil until golden brown, 1 to 2 minutes. (Watch them—broilers are finicky!) Remove the bottom halves of the rolls from the boiler pan. Place the top halves of the rolls, cut sides up, on the broiler pan, and place 2 cheese slices on each roll half to cover. Broil until the cheese melts, about 1 to 2 minutes.

3 Plate the Sloppy Joes by topping each bottom half of roll with ¾ cup meat sauce, ½ cup corn chips, and the top half of the roll.

The more cheese, the better! Don't be shy here!

EXTRA CREDIT!

Melt Velveeta or fondue on top to make it super, super messy!

1 tablespoon kosher salt

1 ½ cups sugar snap peas

4 ounces uncooked spaghetti

¼ cup vegetable oil

1 ½ cups diced thick-cut pancetta or bacon

1 cup yellow onion, diced

2 tablespoons jalapeño chile, seeds removed, diced

¼ cup red chile flakes

2 cups Mama Pat's Meat Sauce (page 137)

1 cup loosely packed chopped fresh flat-leaf parsley

3 large egg yolks

1 tablespoon black pepper

1 cup freshly grated Parmesan cheese

1 tablespoon unsalted butter

1 baguette

I observed the preparation of my first real carbonara while staging (aka cooking for free to learn) for one of my favorite chefs, Suzanne Goin, who had it on the bar menu at her restaurant Lucques. I remember watching the pasta being tossed with fresh peas and bacon and egg yolk and being dazzled by the emulsification process. I break all the rules with this version, which is double meaty, but I hope to capture the same magic!

SPAGHETTI CARBONARA(ISH)

HANDS-ON: 15 MINUTES   TOTAL TIME: 30 MINUTES   SERVES 4

1 Bring a medium pot of salted water to a boil. Blanch the snap peas for 30 seconds. Using a slotted spoon or a small sieve, scoop up the peas, and shock them in a bowl of ice water to retain their color; set aside.

2 Return the water to a boil; add the pasta, and cook until the pasta is al dente, about 10 minutes.

3 Meanwhile, heat the oil in a medium sauté pan over medium-high. Add the pancetta, and cook until crispy, about 5 minutes. Remove the pancetta with a slotted spoon, and transfer to a paper towel-lined plate to drain. Reserve the oil in the pan.

4 Add the drained pancetta, onion, jalapeño, and chile flakes to the pan, and sauté over medium-high, stirring frequently, until the onions start to break down, 3 to 5 minutes. Stir in the meat sauce, reserved peas, and the parsley. Strain the pasta, and add it to the meat sauce along with ¾ cup of the pasta cooking liquid. Mix until all the ingredients are married in the sauté pan.

5 Turn off the heat, and let sit for 1 minute. Stir in the egg yolks and pepper, and mix well. Top with the Parmesan and the butter (do not stir). Cover the pan with a lid, and let sit for another 5 minutes, and then remove the lid and stir to incorporate the melted butter and the cheese. Rip the baguette into "bread fingers," and serve with the carbonara in the pan.

Don't want to blanch? Use thinly shaved raw snap peas or frozen cooked peas.

3

We didn't eat a lot of lasagna when I was a kid; it was mainly a holiday dish. When we did have it, my mother made it with cottage cheese, a comforting choice that I still like using today in combination with the more traditional ricotta. If you have any leftovers, this easy portable dish is great for school or work lunches.

EZ COTTAGE LASAGNA

HANDS-ON: 15 MINUTES   TOTAL TIME: 1 HOUR 15 MINUTES   SERVES 8

1 Preheat the oven to 375°F. Lightly grease a 13- x 9-inch baking dish with nonstick cooking spray. Stir together the cottage cheese, ricotta, egg, basil, salt, and pepper in a medium bowl.

2 Spread 2 cups of Mama Pat's Meat Sauce evenly on the bottom of the prepared baking dish. Place 4 lasagna noodles, overlapping slightly, on the sauce. Top with 1½ cups of the cottage cheese mixture, 4 lasagna noodles, ½ cup of the mozzarella, and 2 cups of the sauce. Top with the remaining 4 lasagna noodles, and press down firmly. Top with the remaining 1½ cups cottage cheese mixture and 2 cups sauce. Coat a piece of aluminum foil with nonstick cooking spray, and cover the dish tightly, cooking spray side down. Bake for 40 minutes.

3 Increase the oven temperature to 425°F. Remove the foil, sprinkle the lasagna with the remaining 2 cups mozzarella, and bake at 425°F until golden brown, 15 to 20 minutes. Garnish with more of the chopped basil.

Freeze the lasagna in serving-sized pieces for portability and easy reheating.

1 ½ cups cottage cheese

1 ½ cups ricotta cheese

1 large egg, beaten

½ cup loosely packed chopped fresh basil, plus additional for garnish

½ teaspoon kosher salt

½ teaspoon black pepper

6 cups Mama Pat's Meat Sauce (page 137)

12 no-boil lasagna noodles

2 ½ cups shredded mozzarella cheese (10 ounces)

EXTRA CREDIT!

Layer seasonal or frozen vegetables in the lasagna, or substitute cooked spinach, chard, or kale leaves for the pasta to create a low-carb meal.

EXTRA CREDIT!

Serve this at a potluck with an elaborate hot sauce and condiment bar.

It takes hours to make great chili, right? Wrong! By making chili with Mama Pat's Meat Sauce (page 137), you've already built up a good 8 hours of flavor that goes straight into this dish. You'll be shocked how quickly this meal is ready. Try this as a topping for baked potatoes or nachos, or as a quesadilla filling.

RYAN'S BEEFY PORK CHILI

HANDS-ON: 35 MINUTES   TOTAL TIME: 35 MINUTES   SERVES 8

1 Cook the sausage, onion, jalapeño, and garlic paste in a Dutch oven or other large heavy-bottomed pot over medium-high, stirring to break the sausage into pieces, until the sausage is browned and crispy, about 10 minutes. Drain the sausage mixture on paper towels; set aside.

2 Reduce the heat to medium. Add the tomato paste, oregano, cumin, garlic salt, paprika, black pepper, and chile flakes to the Dutch oven, and cook over medium until lightly caramelized and darkened, about 5 minutes. Pour in the beer, and stir and scrape to loosen any browned bits from the bottom of the Dutch oven. Return the reserved sausage mixture to the pot along with Mama Pat's Meat Sauce, the diced tomatoes, kidney beans, chickpeas, green chiles, brown sugar, soup base, Worcestershire sauce, and hot sauce, and bring to a boil over medium-high. Reduce the heat to medium-low, and simmer for 5 minutes, or until heated through.

3 To serve, ladle the chili into each of 8 bowls. Stand the tortilla chips in the chili, and serve with the shredded cheese and other desired toppings.

I like the hoppiness of beer for deglazing, but feel free to use water instead (and ship me your beer).

1 pound bulk pork sausage

1 cup diced yellow onion

1 jalapeño chile, seeds removed, finely chopped

1 tablespoon refrigerated garlic paste (from tube)

1 (6-ounce) can tomato paste

2 teaspoons dried oregano

2 teaspoons ground cumin

1 teaspoon garlic salt

1 teaspoon paprika

¾ teaspoon black pepper

¼ to ½ teaspoon red chile flakes

1 ¼ cups beer

3 cups Mama Pat's Meat Sauce (page 137)

1 (28-ounce) can diced tomatoes

1 (16-ounce) can kidney beans, drained

1 (16-ounce) can chickpeas, drained

2 (4-ounce) cans diced green chiles, drained

1 teaspoon light brown sugar

1 teaspoon jarred beef soup base, such as Better Than Bouillon

1 tablespoon Worcestershire sauce

2 dashes of hot sauce, such as Tabasco

1 (13-ounce) package tortilla chips

Shredded Cheddar cheese and chopped scallions or red onion, for topping

5

This nontraditional take on the classic pot pie is an easy way to stretch just 2 cups of sauce, some vegetables, and convenient store-bought buttermilk biscuit dough into a satisfying meal for four. Think of it as an Americana Mama remix! The biscuit-to-pie ratio makes for a very filling dish.

ROGUE POT PIE

HANDS-ON: 25 MINUTES   TOTAL TIME: 45 MINUTES   SERVES 4

2 tablespoons canola oil

1 cup baby carrots, cut on a diagonal into thirds

1 cup diced Yukon Gold potatoes

1 cup diced yellow or white onion

1 cup diced cremini mushrooms

¾ cup diced celery

½ teaspoon kosher salt

4 teaspoons chopped fresh thyme (leave it out if you don't have fresh thyme)

¾ teaspoon black pepper

2 cups Mama Pat's Meat Sauce (page 137)

1 (10.5-ounce) can condensed cream of mushroom soup

1 cup frozen peas

⅓ cup water

1 (16.3-ounce) can refrigerated buttermilk biscuits, such as Pillsbury

1 Preheat the oven to 375°F. Heat the oil in a Dutch oven or large heavy-bottomed pot over medium-high. Add the carrots, potatoes, onion, mushrooms, and celery; cook until the carrots and potatoes are tender, 10 to 12 minutes. Stir in the salt, 3 teaspoons of the thyme, and ½ teaspoon of the pepper; cook 1 minute. Add the meat sauce, mushroom soup, peas, and ⅓ cup water; bring to a boil over medium-high, stirring often. Remove from the heat.

2 Spoon the pot pie filling into an 11- x 7-inch baking dish lightly coated with nonstick cooking spray. Separate the biscuits, and arrange them in a single layer on top of the filling. Sprinkle with the remaining 1 teaspoon thyme and ¼ teaspoon pepper. Put the baking dish on an aluminum foil-lined baking sheet to catch any drips. Bake until the biscuits are golden, about 20 minutes.

POT ROAST

Classic American comfort food starts with a perfect pot roast. You're going to be shocked to see how just a few steps will yield the results you want every single time. And that's just the beginning. Transform this flavorful family favorite into a full beefy repertoire of recipes for busy weekdays you can call your own.

START WITH: 10-HOUR POT ROAST

1 POT ROAST STRUDELS
2 POT ROAST BREAKFAST HASH
3 BEEFY FRENCH DIP-ONION SOUP WITH GRILLED SWISS
   CHEESE SANDWICHES
4 MIAMI SWEATER-WEATHER STEW
5 12-LAYER SUPER NACHOS

This is the quintessential no-fuss slow-cooker dish that is almost too easy to make, yet never fails to impress everyone. If your schedule demands that you can't check on this roast after 10 hours, don't worry; it'll just keep getting better!

10-HOUR POT ROAST

HANDS-ON: 10 MINUTES   TOTAL TIME: 10 HOURS
MAKES 1 ROAST (ABOUT 16 CUPS SHREDDED MEAT)

1 Stir together the dried minced onion, onion powder, garlic powder, pepper, and onion salt in a bowl.

2 Pat the roast dry with a paper towel. Using the back of a spoon or your hands, rub the beef soup base all over the roast. Rub the tomato paste over the roast, and coat with the minced onion mixture.

3 Combine the wine and 1 cup water in a 6-quart slow cooker. Put the roast, fat cap side down, in the slow cooker, and rub the roast with the garlic paste. Top with the chopped onion. Cover and cook on Low until the roast is tender and shreds easily, about 10 hours. Reserve the cooking liquid in an airtight container in the refrigerator—you'll want to use it for the Beefy French Dip-Onion Soup recipe that follows (page 153).

2 tablespoons dried minced onion

1 tablespoon onion powder

1 tablespoon garlic powder

1 tablespoon black pepper

1 ½ teaspoons onion salt

1 (7-pound) top round roast, fat cap intact

2 tablespoons jarred beef soup base, such as Better Than Bouillon

1 (6-ounce) can tomato paste

1 cup dry red wine

1 cup water

2 tablespoons refrigerated garlic paste (from tube)

3 cups chopped yellow onion

1 (17.3-ounce) package frozen puff pastry sheets, thawed

2 tablespoons Dijon mustard

6 Swiss cheese slices

1 tablespoon vegetable oil

7 large eggs

¾ teaspoon kosher salt

½ teaspoon black pepper

¾ cup chopped scallions

1 cup shredded 10-Hour Pot Roast (page 149)

Even though my background is in baking and I firmly believe baking is the most therapeutic thing in the world, I also appreciate premade puff pastry for making creations like this come to life with minimal effort. These fun bites are perfect for breakfast, lunch, dinner, or even a snack.

POT ROAST STRUDELS

HANDS-ON: 30 MINUTES   TOTAL TIME: 1 HOUR 5 MINUTES   SERVES 6

1 Preheat the oven to 400°F. Cut each puff pastry sheet crosswise into thirds. Spread 1 teaspoon Dijon mustard over each puff pastry piece, leaving a 1-inch border on one short side. Tear the Swiss cheese slices in half, and arrange 2 halves over the mustard on each piece of puff pastry piece.

2 Heat the oil in a large nonstick skillet over medium-low. Add 6 of the eggs, the salt, and pepper, and cook, stirring constantly, until very soft curds form, about 4 minutes. Remove from the heat; fold in the scallions. Flatten the egg mixture with a spatula; let cool for 5 minutes.

3 Divide the egg mixture and shredded pot roast evenly among the puff pastry pieces, placing them on top of the cheese. Roll each puff pastry piece from the short end opposite the border, stopping at the border. Beat the remaining egg. Using your fingers, brush each puff pastry border with a small amount of the egg wash. Press to seal, and crimp all exposed edges to enclose the filling and prevent it from spilling out.

4 Place the strudels on a baking sheet. Brush the top of each strudel with the remaining egg wash. Bake until the pastry is cooked through and the edges are golden, about 35 minutes.

These strudels freeze and reheat really well. Wrap them in a damp paper towel, and zap them in the microwave for a minute to bring them back to delicious life.

2

Market & Rye serves many iterations of hash, from chicken to pork to beef. At home, this hash recipe is a great way of utilizing leftovers to make a breakfast (or breakfast as dinner) dish.

POT ROAST BREAKFAST HASH

HANDS-ON: 30 MINUTES   TOTAL TIME: 1 HOUR   SERVES 4

3 cups ½-inch cubes Yukon Gold potatoes

5 tablespoons vegetable oil

2 cups chopped yellow onion

1 tablespoon refrigerated garlic paste (from tube)

1 teaspoon black pepper

1 teaspoon kosher salt

2 cups 10-Hour Pot Roast (page 149), broken into chunks

½ cup chopped fresh flat-leaf parsley, plus more for serving

1 tablespoon prepared horseradish, plus more for serving

1 tablespoon soy sauce

1 tablespoon Worcestershire sauce

¼ cup heavy cream

8 large eggs

8 slices bread of choice, toasted, or 1 baguette, torn and toasted

Sour cream, for serving

Hot sauce, for serving

1 Put the potatoes in a large stockpot filled with cold, salted water. Bring to a boil over high. Reduce the heat to medium-high, and simmer until the potatoes are tender when pierced with a fork, about 10 minutes. Drain and let cool to room temperature.

2 Heat 1 tablespoon of the oil in a large nonstick skillet over medium. Add the onion, garlic paste, pepper, and ¼ teaspoon of the salt; cook, stirring often, until the onions are tender, about 8 minutes.

3 Stir together the onion mixture, chunks of pot roast, ½ cup parsley, 1 tablespoon horseradish, soy sauce, and Worcestershire sauce in a large bowl. Add the potatoes, cream, and remaining ¾ teaspoon salt; stir and mash the potatoes with a wooden spoon until all the ingredients are incorporated. (Some potatoes will be a bit chunky and others completely mashed.)

4 Heat 3 tablespoons of the oil in a large stainless steel or cast-iron skillet over medium-high. Add 4 cups of the potato mixture to the skillet, and flatten with a spatula. Cook, undisturbed, until the bottom starts to crisp, about 2 minutes. Turn the hash over, and flatten with a spatula; cook until a crust has formed on the bottom and around all the edges, about 8 minutes. Remove from the heat.

5 Heat the remaining 1 tablespoon oil in the large nonstick skillet over medium. Break the eggs into the skillet; reduce the heat to medium-low. When the eggs completely detach from the bottom of the skillet, after 2 or 3 minutes, remove the skillet from the heat. Cover and let stand for 2 minutes to finish cooking.

6 Slide the eggs onto the top of the potato hash. Sprinkle with the parsley. Serve with the toast, sour cream, horseradish, and hot sauce.

EXTRA CREDIT!

Make it fiery with Sriracha chili sauce!

I love French dip sandwiches and French onion soup, so in my demented culinary mind I married the two! The dryness of the Swiss for grilled cheese makes the sandwiches super dippable. And the soup requires just 1½ cups of meat, making this meal a super dollar-stretcher. $$

BEEFY FRENCH DIP-ONION SOUP WITH GRILLED SWISS CHEESE SANDWICHES

HANDS-ON: 15 MINUTES   TOTAL TIME: 45 MINUTES   SERVES 4

1 Prepare the soup: Combine the onion, mushrooms, oil, garlic paste, ginger paste, thyme, and 1 teaspoon of the pepper in a stockpot over medium-high. Cover and cook, stirring occasionally, for 10 minutes. Uncover and cook for 10 minutes, stirring occasionally. Add the sherry, stirring to loosen any browned bits from the bottom of the stockpot. Increase the heat to high, and cook until the mixture is syrupy, about 1 minute.

2 Add the cooking liquid, shredded roast, brown sugar, soy sauce, Worcestershire sauce, and remaining 1 teaspoon pepper. Bring to a boil; skim off fat from the top. Remove from the heat, and stir in the scallions.

3 Prepare the sandwiches: Sprinkle the butter pieces evenly on 1 side of the bread slices. Working in batches, microwave the bread on High for 45 seconds.

4 Place 3 cheese slices on the unbuttered side of each of 4 bread slices. Top with the remaining 4 bread slices, buttered side up. Cook the sandwiches, one at a time, in a skillet over medium-high, until golden brown on both sides, 3 to 5 minutes per side. Set aside on a platter.

5 Ladle 2 cups of the soup into each of 4 bowls. Top with the grated Parmesan; serve with the hot sandwiches.

SOUP

6 cups thinly sliced yellow onion

3 cups cremini mushrooms, quartered

¼ cup vegetable oil

2 tablespoons refrigerated garlic paste (from tube)

1 tablespoon refrigerated ginger paste (from tube)

1 tablespoon chopped fresh thyme

2 teaspoons black pepper

1 cup sherry

6 cups cooking liquid from 10-Hour Pot Roast (page 149)

1 ½ cups shredded 10-Hour Pot Roast (page 149)

2 teaspoons light brown sugar

2 teaspoons soy sauce

1 teaspoon Worcestershire sauce

¾ cup chopped scallions

SANDWICHES

2 tablespoons unsalted butter, cut into pieces

8 slices bread, such as sourdough, white, or whole wheat

12 slices Swiss cheese

¼ cup freshly grated Parmesan cheese (about 1 ounce)

Every year Lesley and I go to Miami, where I became hooked on a robust Cuban specialty called *ropa vieja.* This stew is loosely inspired by this traditional dish and the plantains that usually accompany it, though I've opted for sweeter bananas and more of a West Coast vibe. Since you already slow-cooked the pot roast, you don't have to spend hours braising the meat like you typically would to enjoy some *ropa.*

MIAMI SWEATER-WEATHER STEW

HANDS-ON: 5 MINUTES   TOTAL TIME: 20 MINUTES   SERVES 4

1 Heat the oil in a large skillet or Dutch oven over high. Add the banana slices, and cook, stirring often, until golden brown on all sides, about 4 minutes. Transfer the banana slices to a plate; sprinkle with ½ teaspoon each of the cumin and salt.

2 Reduce the heat to medium-low, and add the onion to the skillet. Cook, stirring occasionally, until caramelized, about 10 minutes. Stir in the garlic paste, tomato paste, black pepper, crushed red pepper, and remaining 1 teaspoon each cumin and salt; cook until fragrant, about 1 minute.

3 Add the shredded pot roast, chicken stock, roasted red peppers, tomato sauce, vinegar, and hot sauce. Increase the heat to high, and bring to a boil, stirring occasionally. Remove from the heat; stir in the olives. Serve the stew over the rice with the bananas and a spoonful of chili paste on the side. Sprinkle each serving with the cilantro.

¼ cup vegetable oil

3 ripe bananas, each cut crosswise into 6 slices

1 ½ teaspoons ground cumin

1 ½ teaspoons kosher salt

2 cups minced yellow onion

3 tablespoons refrigerated garlic paste (from tube)

1 tablespoon tomato paste

1 teaspoon black pepper

¼ teaspoon crushed red pepper

4 cups shredded 10-Hour Pot Roast (page 149)

3 cups chicken stock

2 cups jarred roasted sliced red bell peppers

1 (5-ounce) can tomato sauce

2 teaspoons red wine vinegar

4 dashes of hot sauce, such as Tabasco

¾ cup sliced pimiento-stuffed green olives

2 cups microwaveable jasmine rice (from pouch), microwaved according to package directions

Refrigerated chili paste (from tube), for serving

½ cup chopped fresh cilantro

5

Now let's bring the traditional American pot roast south of the border with a macho take on Mexican nachos that promises to be the center of attention. It's hard to go back to regular nachos once you've had a taste of this super style.

12-LAYER SUPER NACHOS

HANDS-ON: 10 MINUTES   TOTAL TIME: 22 MINUTES   SERVES 4

2 cups shredded 10-Hour Pot Roast (page 149)

1 cup water

2 teaspoons taco seasoning mix

1 (16-ounce) can refried beans

1 (7-ounce) can diced green chiles

5 cups tortilla chips

2 cups Cheddar cheese, grated (about 8 ounces)

1 (4-ounce) can sliced black olives, drained

½ cup diced tomato

½ cup loosely packed roughly chopped fresh cilantro

½ cup roughly chopped scallions

¼ cup sour cream

1 ripe avocado, pitted, peeled, and cubed

¼ cup jarred or fresh salsa

½ cup pickled jalapeño chile slices

¼ cup diced red onion

1 Preheat a broiler, arranging a rack 6 inches from the heat source. Combine the shredded roast, 1 cup water, and taco seasoning mix in a skillet over medium-high. Cook until the liquid evaporates, about 5 minutes.

2 Stir together the beans and green chiles in a microwave-safe bowl; cover with a damp paper towel, and microwave on High until heated through, about 4 minutes. Spread the bean mixture evenly in the bottom of a 9-inch pie pan. Stand the tortilla chips in the bean mixture like soldiers. Scatter the shredded roast mixture over and around the chips, filling every crevice. Top with the Cheddar. Broil until the nachos are a bubbly mess, about 3 minutes. Remove from the oven.

3 Top the nachos with the olives, tomato, cilantro, and scallions. Dollop the sour cream in the center; arrange the avocado and salsa around the sour cream. Sprinkle with the pickled jalapeños and the red onion. Put the pie pan on a platter for serving—so eaters can be messy.

EXTRA CREDIT!

Transform these nachos into a taco salad with the lettuce of your choice (iceberg works well).

FROZEN CORN

Corn is one of the only frozen ingredients that, once reheated, doesn't taste like it's been frozen. Carrots get crystallized and peas can become gummy and pasty, but the flavor and texture of corn hold up very well in a deep freeze.

If you are lucky enough to have access to fresh corn, feel free to use it in these recipes (A 16-ounce package of frozen corn is about 3 cups of fresh kernels), but using frozen corn is quicker than cutting it off the cob. And that's time you can use to do something more fun instead!

The next time you have a deep craving for something fried, these hushpuppies are just the thing! The green chiles are fairly mild but contribute a subtle heat that makes these light, airy nibbles especially addicting.

GREEN CHILE HUSHPUPPIES

HANDS-ON: 15 MINUTES   TOTAL TIME: 45 MINUTES   SERVES 16

1 Pour the oil to a depth of 2 inches in a large Dutch oven or large heavy skillet, and heat over high until the oil reaches 375°F on a candy thermometer.

2 Meanwhile, whisk together the milk, cream, corn, onion, eggs, green chiles, hot sauce, and lemon juice in a medium bowl.

3 Stir together the cornmeal, flour, salt, baking powder, sugar, and baking soda in another medium bowl until evenly incorporated. Fold the corn mixture into the dry ingredients.

4 Using a small (2-tablespoon) ice-cream scoop, scoop and drop the corn batter into the hot oil in batches. Fry the hushpuppies until golden, about 2 minutes. (Stir the batter remaining in the bowl between batches; the recipe makes about 64 hushpuppies total.) Drain the hushpuppies on a plate lined with paper towels, and blot them with more paper towels. Serve immediately.

Vegetable oil

1 ¼ cups whole milk

1 ¼ cups heavy cream

1 cup frozen petite corn, thawed and drained

⅓ cup grated yellow onion (with juice)

3 large eggs

2 (4-ounce) cans diced green chiles, drained

1 tablespoon green hot sauce, such as green Tabasco

1 teaspoon fresh lemon juice

2 ½ cups plain yellow cornmeal

2 cups all-purpose flour

1 tablespoon kosher salt

2 teaspoons baking powder

1 teaspoon sugar

1 teaspoon baking soda

2

1 ½ cups uncooked quinoa

¾ cup, plus 2 tablespoons vegetable oil

1 tablespoon kosher salt

1 ½ cups, plus ⅓ cup water

4 cups frozen petite corn, thawed and drained

1 (15-ounce) can brown lentils, drained and rinsed

½ cup red wine vinegar

¼ cup Dijon mustard

1 teaspoon black pepper

1 teaspoon honey

2 dashes of hot sauce, such as Tabasco

4 ounces crumbled feta cheese (about 1 cup)

1 cup toasted slivered almonds

½ cup loosely packed fresh flat-leaf parsley, chopped

½ cup chopped fresh chives

When I got my first chef job at Myth Cafe in San Francisco, this was the first salad I put on the menu. We peeled and shucked fresh corn that we'd get in daily from a local farm, and my salad cook hated me because we'd sell 40 to 60 orders a day. I once made this salad with Hoda Kotb and Kathie Lee Gifford live, on the TODAY show, and you woulda thought I'd have given them one of Oprah's favorite things or a new Mercedes, they loved it so much! This is a must-try dish.

CORN, QUINOA, AND FETA SALAD WITH RED WINE VINAIGRETTE

HANDS-ON: 15 MINUTES   TOTAL TIME: 45 MINUTES   SERVES 8

1 Preheat the oven to 375°F. Combine the quinoa, 1 tablespoon of the oil, and 1 teaspoon of the salt in an ovenproof saucepan over low, and cook, stirring constantly, just until the quinoa begins to pop like popcorn, about 8 minutes. Increase the heat; stir in 1 ½ cups of the water, and bring to a boil. Remove the pan from the heat; cover and bake until all the water is absorbed and the quinoa is cooked, 20 to 25 minutes. Remove the pan from the oven; uncover and let stand for 5 minutes. Fluff with a fork.

2 Heat 1 tablespoon of the oil in a medium skillet over medium-high; add the corn, and cook without stirring until the corn is golden and crispy on one side, 8 to 10 minutes. Stir the corn and lentils into the quinoa.

3 Process the vinegar, mustard, pepper, honey, hot sauce, and remaining ¾ cup oil, ⅓ cup water, and remaining 2 teaspoons salt in a food processor until emulsified. Drizzle ½ cup of the vinaigrette onto the sides of a serving bowl; add the quinoa mixture, and toss it into the sides of the bowl to coat with the vinaigrette. Add the feta, almonds, parsley, and chives, and stir just until incorporated.

Store any remaining vinaigrette in an airtight container in the refrigerator for up to 1 week.

2 tablespoons vegetable oil

6 slices turkey bacon, cut into 1-inch pieces

2 cups frozen petite corn, thawed and drained

½ cup minced yellow onion

2 jalapeño chiles, seeds removed, chopped

10 large eggs

½ teaspoon kosher salt

½ teaspoon black pepper

4 ounces goat cheese, cut or torn into large pieces

1 ripe avocado, sliced

Chopped fresh chives, for serving

The test of a true chef is whether you have the patience, time and accuracy to pull off a stellar omelette. But the omelette that I make for my wife is the lazy man's version because I just cook it in a skillet until the eggs and other ingredients come together, and then pop it into the oven to bake.

LESLEY'S CORN AND TURKEY BACON FRITTATA

HANDS-ON: 10 MINUTES   TOTAL TIME: 30 MINUTES   SERVES 4

1 Preheat the oven to 375°F. Heat the oil in an ovenproof nonstick skillet over medium-high; add the turkey bacon, corn, onion, and jalapeño, and cook, stirring often and turning the bacon frequently, until the onions are caramelized and the bacon looks almost too crispy, 6 to 8 minutes. Remove the skillet from the heat.

2 Whisk together the eggs, salt, and pepper. Pour the egg mixture over the corn mixture in the skillet, and return the skillet to medium-high. Without stirring, allow the mixture to start to set on the sides of the skillet. Gently pull the egg mixture from the sides into the center of the skillet, moving the egg mixture around; cook until it starts to set, about 1 minute. Remove from the heat; dot the top with the goat cheese pieces.

3 Bake until the eggs are set, about 10 minutes. Run a spatula under and around the sides of the pan to loosen the frittata. Top with the avocado slices and chives before serving.

Make sure your add-in ingredients are thoroughly cooked because you can't rely on the oven time to cook them.

I first came up with this soup in the summer because we had an abundance of corn at my restaurant. Customers began to ask for it year-round, though, so I developed this version using frozen corn. I love how effortless it is to make, and it's always a crowd pleaser.

YEAR-ROUND SWEET CORN SOUP

HANDS-ON: 15 MINUTES   TOTAL TIME: 55 MINUTES   SERVES 10

1 Heat the oil and butter in a Dutch oven or large heavy-bottomed pot over medium-low. Add the leeks, onion, garlic paste, and salt, and cook until the vegetables are tender, about 20 minutes, stirring once or twice. Add the corn, vegetable stock, and cream, and simmer about 20 minutes, stirring once or twice. (Do not allow the soup to come to a boil.)

2 Using a handheld (immersion) blender, process the vegetable mixture in the pot until smooth. Sprinkle the soup with the chives. Serve each cup of soup with a dollop of sour cream and a drizzle of Sriracha.

If you don't own a handheld blender, you can use a regular blender. Working in batches, transfer the corn mixture to the blender, removing the central piece of the blender lid to allow steam to escape, and secure the lid on the blender. Put a clean dish towel over the lid opening, and process until the soup is smooth. Repeat with the remaining corn mixture.

3 tablespoons vegetable oil

2 tablespoons unsalted butter

4 cups diced leeks

4 cups diced yellow onion

2 tablespoons refrigerated garlic paste (from tube)

1 tablespoon kosher salt

4 cups frozen petite corn, thawed and drained

4 cups vegetable stock

1 cup heavy cream

Minced fresh chives

Sour cream, for serving

Sriracha chili sauce or Asian chili oil, for serving

EXTRA CREDIT!

Try different toppings or serve the soup over penne or ravioli with crispy pancetta or bacon, or as a summertime sauce for chicken.

My good friend Carla Hall first introduced me to johnnycakes one year as we cooked together in Yosemite National Park. Her take was Jamaican style and served with black beans, and I got so excited by this combination that I had to create my own spin. I think that mine are more on the savory side, with a little kick.

CORN, JALAPEÑO, AND CHIVE JOHNNYCAKES

HANDS-ON: 15 MINUTES   TOTAL TIME: 45 MINUTES   SERVES 6

1 Stir together the corn, cornmeal, boiling water, jalapeño, sugar, salt, and pepper until well combined. Cover and chill for 30 minutes.

2 Heat the butter and the oil in a medium skillet over medium. Working in batches of 4 to 6 johnnycakes, drop ¼-cup scoops of the batter into the hot butter mixture, and cook until golden, 3 to 5 minutes per side. Transfer to a platter, sprinkle with some of the chives, and set aside while you cook the remaining batter.

3 Drizzle the maple syrup on each serving plate, and sprinkle with a couple dashes of the hot sauce. Top with the hot johnnycakes, and serve immediately.

4 cups frozen petite corn, thawed and drained

2 cups fine yellow cornmeal

2 cups boiling water

1 jalapeño chile, seeds removed, diced

2 teaspoons sugar

1 ½ teaspoons kosher salt

1 teaspoon black pepper

2 tablespoons unsalted butter

2 tablespoons vegetable oil

2 tablespoons finely chopped fresh chives

Maple syrup

Hot sauce, such as Tabasco

FROZEN SHRIMP

I think you'll be pleasantly surprised at how many different dishes you can easily make out of a simple bag of frozen shrimp. We're talking total seafood satisfaction! All that's needed is to defrost and rinse them and you'll be on your way to making summery shrimp cakes, a sweet and garlicky California-Asian creation, succulent scampi, the easiest stir-fry ever, and a healthy lettuce-wrapped dish.

HASSLE-FREE SHRIMP

I like using 2-pound bags that contain 26 to 30 frozen shrimp per pound so you get decent-sized specimens, but feel free to select whatever size shrimp you like as long as you make sure they've been peeled and deveined—it's a real time-saver. Thaw the package overnight in the fridge, or place the whole package (without opening) in room-temperature water for 15 to 20 minutes. Drain and rinse the shrimp in a colander. Now you're ready to tackle the FIVE!

START WITH: PEELED, DEVEINED, TAIL-OFF FROZEN SHRIMP

1 SHRIMP CAKES WITH CUCUMBER-AVOCADO SALAD
2 EASIEST SHRIMP STIR-FRY
3 MANGO SHRIMP LETTUCE CUPS
4 CALIFORNIA SWEET GARLIC-ALMOND SHRIMP
5 DANNY'S LEMON-PEPPER SCAMPI

I first came up with these shrimp cakes for the catering side of my company. They're always a home run. They almost fall apart because they're barely bound together. But because they aren't bready, they have awesome flavor. The accompanying salad is crunchy and refreshing, and it's dressed with a creative take on tartar sauce. There are a lot of ingredients here, but don't be intimidated. It's really a 1-2-3-go kind of dish.

SHRIMP CAKES WITH CUCUMBER-AVOCADO SALAD

HANDS-ON: 20 MINUTES   TOTAL TIME: 1 HOUR   SERVES 6

1 Prepare the shrimp cakes: Heat 2 tablespoons of the oil in a large nonstick skillet over medium-high. Cook the bell peppers, ginger paste, and garlic paste in the hot oil, stirring often, until the bell peppers are tender, about 10 minutes. Remove from the heat, and let cool for 5 minutes.

2 Transfer the bell pepper mixture to a medium bowl, and stir in the scallions, cilantro, soy sauce, Old Bay, black pepper, lemon zest, egg white, hot sauce, and 2 tablespoons of the sesame seeds. Add half of the chopped shrimp. Place the other half of the shrimp in a food processor, and process until finely chopped. Transfer to the bowl with the shrimp cake mixture. Add ½ cup of the panko, and stir to combine. (Or feel free to use your hands.) Chill for 10 to 15 minutes.

3 Stir together the remaining 1 cup panko and 4 tablespoons toasted sesame seeds in a shallow dish. Using a ½-cup measure, scoop the shrimp cake mixture and pack it in tightly to get out any air pockets. Flip the scoop onto a plate or cutting board, and press down to flatten it into a ½-inch-thick cake. Repeat the procedure with the remaining shrimp cake mixture. Place the cakes in the panko mixture, coating both sides. Heat the remaining 2 tablespoons oil in the large nonstick skillet over medium-low. Cook the cakes in the hot oil until browned and cooked through, about 5 minutes on each side. Transfer to a plate lined with paper towels; drain.

continued

SHRIMP CAKES

4 tablespoons corn oil

1 cup diced yellow bell pepper

1 cup diced red bell pepper

1 tablespoon refrigerated ginger paste (from tube)

1 tablespoon refrigerated garlic paste (from tube)

1 cup chopped scallions

½ cup chopped fresh cilantro

1 tablespoon soy sauce

1 teaspoon Old Bay seasoning

1 teaspoon black pepper

1 teaspoon lemon zest

1 large egg white

3 dashes of hot sauce, such as Tabasco

6 tablespoons toasted sesame seeds

2 cups frozen shrimp (page 169), thawed, patted dry with paper towels, chopped

1½ cups panko (Japanese-style breadcrumbs)

SHRIMP CAKES WITH CUCUMBER-AVOCADO SALAD
continued

SALAD

1 cup seeded diced cucumber

½ teaspoon kosher salt

¾ cup red radishes, sliced

¾ cup thinly sliced sugar snap peas

1 avocado, pitted, peeled, and cubed

½ cup peeled diced jicama

½ cup mayonnaise

1 tablespoon fresh lemon juice

1 teaspoon soy sauce

½ teaspoon black pepper

6 red leaf or other crunchy lettuce leaves

4 Prepare the salad: Toss the cucumber with ¼ teaspoon of the salt; drain in a colander for 15 minutes, and pat dry with paper towels. Stir together the cucumber, radishes, snap peas, avocado, jicama, mayonnaise, lemon juice, soy sauce, black pepper, and remaining ¼ teaspoon salt in a medium bowl. Place each shrimp cake on a lettuce leaf, and top with a few spoonfuls of the cucumber-avocado salad.

Don't want to use oil? Pan-sear the shrimp cakes and pop them in a preheated 350°F oven for 10 to 15 minutes instead.

EXTRA CREDIT!

Crumble the shrimp cakes up and toss them in a salad, or make mini sliders topped with crushed avocado.

Made with both frozen and microwaveable ingredients, this stir-fry is quick, easy, and truly value stretching. This is a meal that requires just two bowls for prepping and one pan for cooking. It teaches you how to cook a little strategically—there's minimal mess if you think it through. This is one of my favorite go-tos because I love microwaveable rice, as you'll see in the Brown Rice section (page 180).

EASIEST SHRIMP STIR-FRY

HANDS-ON: 10 MINUTES   TOTAL TIME: 25 MINUTES   SERVES 4

1 Stir together the garlic paste, ginger paste, and 1 tablespoon of the soy sauce in a medium bowl. Add the shrimp, and stir to coat. Let stand for 15 minutes.

2 Heat 3 tablespoons of the oil in a large skillet over high. Add the broccoli slaw and onion; cook until lightly browned, about 7 minutes.

3 Add the prepared rice to the skillet, and toast over high until golden, about 4 minutes. Transfer the rice and vegetables to a small bowl. Add the shrimp and remaining 1 tablespoon oil to the skillet, stir once, and cook for about 1 minute. Stir in the rice, vegetables, 1 teaspoon Sriracha, and remaining 1 tablespoon soy sauce. Cook until the rice snaps, crackles, and pops, about 1 minute. Serve garnished with the cilantro and lime wedges, and additional Sriracha.

2 tablespoons refrigerated garlic paste (from tube)

2 tablespoons refrigerated ginger paste (from tube)

2 tablespoons soy sauce

2 cups frozen shrimp (page 169), thawed, patted dry with paper towels, cut in half

4 tablespoons corn oil

2 cups broccoli slaw or cabbage slaw (shredded carrots, broccoli, and red cabbage)

1 cup minced yellow onion

1 ½ cups microwaveable brown rice, microwaved according to package directions

1 teaspoon Sriracha chili sauce, plus more for serving

Chopped fresh cilantro, for garnish

Lime wedges, for garnish

EXTRA CREDIT!

Use my Broccoli-Kale Slaw (page 47), minus the dressing, instead of store-bought slaw.

EXTRA CREDIT!

Add apple and/or crunchy wonton skins to the mix to up the crunch factor.

Think of this dish as a healthy play on shrimp tacos with mango salsa, where the butter lettuce replaces tortillas to serve as a low-carb wrapper. A portable, assemble-it-yourself recipe, it's fun to serve to people of all ages. There are actually two fruits in the mix here; did you know that avocado is a fruit? Great for lunch, dinner, or that winning party appetizer.

MANGO-SHRIMP LETTUCE CUPS

HANDS-ON: 10 MINUTES   TOTAL TIME: 35 MINUTES   SERVES 6

1 Stir together the onion, orange juice, ginger paste, garlic paste, chili paste, soy sauce, and vinegar in a medium bowl. Add the shrimp; stir to coat, and let stand for 15 minutes.

2 Stir together the cucumber, mango, avocado, jicama, cilantro, lime juice, and salt in another bowl.

3 Heat the oil in a large skillet over high. Cook the shrimp on one side just until the shrimp turn pink, 3 to 4 minutes. Toss the shrimp with the mango salsa, and chill for 10 to 15 minutes. Serve at room temperature with the lettuce leaves.

½ cup minced red onion

¼ cup orange juice

2 tablespoons refrigerated ginger paste (from tube)

1 tablespoon refrigerated garlic paste (from tube)

1 tablespoon Asian chili paste (sambal oelek)

1 tablespoon soy sauce

1 tablespoon red wine vinegar

2 cups frozen shrimp (page 169), thawed, patted dry with paper towels, chopped

1 medium cucumber, peeled, seeded, and diced (about 1 ½ cups)

1 cup diced mango

1 ripe avocado, pitted, peeled, and diced

½ cup peeled and chopped jicama

¼ cup roughly chopped fresh cilantro leaves

3 tablespoons fresh lime juice

¼ teaspoon kosher salt

1 tablespoon canola oil

1 head butter lettuce, leaves separated

This dish is a homage to my good friend Martin Yan, a chef and television personality who has done a lot to bring Asian cuisine and culture into American kitchens. He serves an amazing version of classic honey-walnut shrimp at his San Francisco restaurant M.Y. China, which is where I first fell in love with it. My spin on Martin's dish is a California boy's take with garlic and candied almonds, two Central Valley exports.

CALIFORNIA SWEET GARLIC-ALMOND SHRIMP

HANDS-ON: 15 MINUTES   TOTAL TIME: 15 MINUTES   SERVES 6

1 Prepare the candied almonds: Bring the sugar, ½ cup water, and honey to a boil in a small nonstick saucepan over high. Cook until the mixture turns a golden caramel color, about 8 minutes. Remove from the heat, and stir in the almonds to coat. Spread the almonds on a plate coated with nonstick cooking spray; cool for about 10 minutes. Roughly chop the almonds with a chef's knife.

2 Prepare the sweet garlic shrimp: Using your hands, combine the shrimp, garlic paste, salt, and pepper in a medium bowl. Let stand for 5 minutes.

3 Put the beaten egg whites in a shallow dish. Put the cornstarch in another shallow dish. Dip each shrimp into the egg whites, shaking off the excess; dredge in the cornstarch.

4 Heat the oil in a large, deep nonstick skillet over medium-high until a deep-fry thermometer reads 375°F. Fry the shrimp in batches until golden brown, 30 to 45 seconds each. (Don't overcook or you'll end up with rubber bands!) Transfer to a plate lined with paper towels.

5 Stir together the mayonnaise, condensed milk, and honey in a large bowl. Add the shrimp, and toss to coat. Sprinkle with the scallions, sesame seeds, and ½ cup of the almonds. Serve with the lime wedges.

CANDIED ALMONDS

½ cup granulated sugar

½ cup water

1 tablespoon honey

1 cup whole blanched almonds

SWEET GARLIC SHRIMP

1 ¾ cups frozen shrimp (page 169), thawed, patted dry with paper towels

2 tablespoons refrigerated garlic paste (from tube)

1 teaspoon kosher salt

1 teaspoon black pepper

3 large egg whites, beaten

¾ cup cornstarch

1 cup corn oil

¼ cup mayonnaise

1 tablespoon sweetened condensed milk

1 teaspoon honey

¼ cup sliced scallions

1 tablespoon toasted sesame seeds

Lime wedges, for serving

5

2 tablespoons refrigerated garlic paste
(from tube)

1 teaspoon Dijon mustard

1 teaspoon garlic salt

1 teaspoon lemon pepper

2 cups frozen shrimp (page 169),
thawed, patted dry with
paper towels

3 tablespoons corn oil

2 tablespoons fresh lemon juice

6 tablespoons chopped fresh flat-leaf
parsley

½ cup diced yellow onion

1 tablespoon brined capers, drained
and minced

1 cup dry white wine

1 cup bottled clam juice

1 cup heavy cream

½ cup cherry tomatoes (about
7 tomatoes), quartered

2 ounces (¼ cup) cold butter, quartered

Baguette, for serving

Shrimp scampi is my stepdad Danny's go-to dish—I'm pretty sure he wooed my mother with it, and they've been together for more than 15 years! This version is a lot of Danny and a little bit of me, inspired by tips and tricks I've learned along the way. That includes the best way to sear shrimp, which you're about to discover. (Spoiler: Sear them on one side only so they don't get rubbery!)

DANNY'S LEMON-PEPPER SCAMPI

HANDS-ON: 15 MINUTES   TOTAL TIME: 27 MINUTES   SERVES 4

1 Stir together the garlic paste, mustard, garlic salt, and lemon pepper in a medium bowl. Add the shrimp, stirring to coat, and let stand for 5 to 10 minutes.

2 Heat 2 tablespoons of the oil in a large skillet over high. Place the shrimp in a single layer in the hot skillet; cook for 1 minute on one side. Return the shrimp to the bowl with the marinade. Add the lemon juice and 4 tablespoons of the parsley; stir and set aside.

3 Put the onion, capers, and remaining 1 tablespoon oil in the skillet. Cook over medium-high until the onion is tender, about 5 minutes. Add the wine, clam juice, and cream, and boil until reduced by half, about 5 minutes, adding the tomatoes during the last 3 minutes of cooking. (You can always add water if the mixture seems too thick.)

4 Remove from the heat. Add the shrimp mixture, and stir. Whisk in the butter until melted. Stir in the remaining 2 tablespoons parsley. Serve with torn pieces of baguette or grilled bread.

If you don't have a large skillet, sear the shrimp in batches.

EXTRA CREDIT!

Use a red wine like Pinot Noir instead of white wine for a sexy rouge sauce.

BROWN RICE

There are countless cookbooks available that will teach you how to labor over the perfect pot of rice. This is not one of those books! ☺ Microwaveable brown rice is way too convenient and satisfying not to use on a regular basis, especially when you learn how many great meals you can make with it. If this is your first time using precooked rice, I'm here to absolve you of any guilt you may feel if you never go back to boiling rice again.

START WITH: PRECOOKED BROWN RICE

1 VERY BERRY WARM MUESLI
2 GREEK WATERMELON-RICE SALAD
3 KIELBASA, KALE, AND BROWN RICE SOUP
4 BROWN RICE-STUFFED CABBAGE ROLLS
5 CHOCOLATE-COCONUT RICE PUDDING

Kristin Kolnacki, a plant-based pastry chef in New York City, first turned me on to the potential of muesli when we worked together at the old Myth Cafe in San Francisco. Typically, people make muesli overnight in the fridge, but you can achieve instant gratification with this method.

VERY BERRY WARM MUESLI

HANDS-ON: 5 MINUTES   TOTAL TIME: 5 MINUTES   SERVES 6

2 teaspoons light brown sugar

½ teaspoon kosher salt

2 cups whole milk

1 (10-ounce) pouch (about 2 cups) precooked brown rice microwaved according to package directions

1 cup granola of your choice

½ cup dried cranberries

½ cup walnut pieces, crushed

1 tablespoon unsalted butter

1 tablespoon creamy peanut butter

1 ½ to 2 cups plain fat-free Greek yogurt

3 bananas, sliced, for serving

1 cup fresh raspberries, for serving

1 Whisk together the brown sugar, salt, and 1 cup of the milk in a medium saucepan over medium-high, and bring to a boil. Add the prepared rice, and cook until the mixture has reduced to a slightly soupy consistency, about 2 minutes. Remove from the heat, and stir in the granola, cranberries, walnuts, butter, and peanut butter. Add the remaining 1 cup milk, return to a boil over medium-high, and cook until the muesli thickens, about 30 seconds. Remove from the heat, and cover until ready to serve.

2 Fill each of 6 bowls with about ¼ cup yogurt on one side and ½ cup muesli on the other side. Top each serving with a portion of the banana slices and 4 or 5 fresh raspberries. Serve immediately.

If you want to make more of a porridge, add an additional cup of milk in the second stage of cooking.

If you know me, you know of my extreme fondness for Greek and Mediterranean cuisine, so it would be a sin not to include a Greek salad in this book. You may think I'm weird to use watermelon here, but I found out by accident that it works really well in this salad. As for the dressing, I think I've won over more people with this vinaigrette than pretty much anything else I've created to date.

GREEK WATERMELON-RICE SALAD

HANDS-ON: 20 MINUTES   TOTAL TIME: 20 MINUTES   SERVES 8

1 Prepare the vinaigrette: Process the mint, cilantro, oil, lemon juice, garlic paste, jalapeño, capers with juice, salt, and pepper in a blender until smooth.

2 Prepare the salad: Toss together the rice, cucumbers, tomatoes, watermelon, olives, onion, and 1 cup of the vinaigrette in a large bowl. (Reserve the remaining 2 cups vinaigrette for another use; it may be stored in the refrigerator for up to 2 days.) Top the salad with the feta cheese; sprinkle with the salt and pepper.

VINAIGRETTE (makes about 3 cups)

2 cups loosely packed fresh mint leaves

1 cup loosely packed fresh cilantro leaves

2 cups extra-virgin olive oil

1 cup fresh lemon juice

3 tablespoons refrigerated garlic paste (from tube)

1 jalapeño chile, seeds removed, diced

1 tablespoon brined capers with juice

1 tablespoon kosher salt

2 teaspoons black pepper

SALAD

1 (10-ounce) pouch (about 2 cups) precooked brown rice microwaved according to package instructions

2 English cucumber, seeds removed, chopped (about 2 cups)

2 cups halved cherry tomatoes

1 cup diced watermelon (seeds removed)

1 cup halved pitted Kalamata olives

½ cup thinly sliced red onion

1 cup crumbled feta cheese (4 ounces)

½ teaspoon kosher salt

½ teaspoon black pepper

Soup doesn't get much more comforting than this! My creation is an ode to two dishes that I love: one Mama Pat made for us regularly that combined potatoes and peppers with turkey kielbasa, and a hearty Portuguese soup from a San Francisco restaurant called Grubstake that has cured many of my late-night hunger cravings.

KIELBASA, KALE, AND BROWN RICE SOUP

HANDS-ON: 15 MINUTES   TOTAL TIME: 45 MINUTES   SERVES 10

¼ cup vegetable oil

2 cups diced turkey kielbasa sausage (about 8 ounces)

2 (15-ounce) cans peeled whole white potatoes

3 cups minced yellow onion

1 jalapeño chile, seeds removed, diced

1 ½ tablespoons jarred chicken stock base, such as Better Than Bouillon

1 tablespoon minced fresh garlic

8 cups water

1 bunch kale, stems removed, chopped (about 6 cups)

1 (10-ounce) pouch (about 2 cups) precooked brown rice straight from the freezer (do not microwave)

1 tablespoon fresh lemon juice

1 teaspoon black pepper

½ teaspoon kosher salt

1 Heat the oil in a stockpot over medium-high. Add the kielbasa, and cook until it starts to caramelize, about 5 minutes. Transfer the kielbasa to a paper towel–lined plate to drain. Reduce the heat to medium, add the potatoes, onion, jalapeño, stock base, and garlic, and cook, stirring occasionally, until the potatoes are tender, 8 to 10 minutes. Add 8 cups water, and bring to a boil over high. Remove the stockpot from the heat.

2 Working in batches, carefully transfer the hot soup to a blender, and process until smooth. Return the pureed soup to the pot, and bring to a boil over medium-high. Add the reserved kielbasa, kale, rice, lemon juice, pepper, and salt, and cook until warmed through, 5 to 10 minutes.

For a richer flavor, substitute pork kielbasa for the turkey version.

4

1 medium head cabbage

¼ cup vegetable oil

3 cups diced yellow onion

3 tablespoons refrigerated garlic paste
(from tube)

3 tablespoons tomato paste

1 cup dry white wine

1 pound bulk pork sausage

1 pound ground beef

1 (10-ounce) pouch (about 2 cups)
precooked brown rice straight from
the freezer (do not microwave)

½ cup loosely packed fresh flat-leaf
parsley leaves, chopped

1 large egg

1 ½ tablespoons kosher salt

1 tablespoon Dijon mustard

1 teaspoon Asian chili paste
(sambal oelek)

1 teaspoon black pepper

½ teaspoon creamy horseradish sauce

1 (24-ounce) jar marinara sauce

1 cup freshly grated Parmesan cheese
(4 ounces)

We didn't cook with cabbage growing up; we only saw it drowning in mayo in KFC coleslaw. It wasn't until I took a German cooking class in college that I learned there were other uses for cabbage.

BROWN RICE–STUFFED CABBAGE ROLLS

HANDS-ON: 20 MINUTES   **TOTAL TIME: 1 HOUR 5 MINUTES**   **SERVES 6**

1 Bring a few inches of water to a boil in a stockpot. Cut the cabbage in half lengthwise, and cut out and discard a round from the core of the cabbage. Place the cabbage, core side down, in a steamer basket over the boiling water. Cover and steam until the leaves are tender, 10 to 15 minutes. Transfer the cabbage to a plate to cool.

2 Preheat the oven to 425°F. Heat the oil in a large Dutch oven over medium-high. Add the onion and garlic paste, and cook, stirring occasionally, until golden, about 5 minutes. Increase the heat to high; add the tomato paste, and stir until the mixture is sticky and smells rich, 2 to 3 minutes. Stir in the wine, and cook until it evaporates, about 30 seconds. Remove from the heat; let cool for 5 to 10 minutes.

3 Remove the cabbage leaves that are too small to use for rolls; chop them and put them in a large bowl. Add the sausage, beef, rice, parsley, egg, salt, mustard, chili paste, pepper, and horseradish; mix until thoroughly combined. Stir in the cooled onion mixture. Using a spoon or ice cream scoop, form 12 football-shaped meatballs (about ¾ cup each).

4 Spread 1 ½ cups of the marinara in the bottom of a 13- x 9-inch baking dish. Place a meatball in the center of 1 or 2 layers of cabbage leaves, and wrap the leaves around the meatball. Repeat with the remaining meatballs and cabbage leaves. Arrange the cabbage rolls, seam sides down, in rows in the prepared dish. Cover the rolls with the remaining marinara sauce. Cover the dish with plastic wrap, and then with aluminum foil, dull side up. Bake the cabbage rolls for 45 minutes. Remove the baking dish from the oven, and increase the heat to broil. Remove and discard the foil and plastic wrap. Sprinkle the cabbage rolls with the Parmesan, and broil 6 inches from the heat source until golden, about 2 minutes.

This is an exceptionally easy dessert to make, but don't walk away while you're doing it. Coconut milk boils over easily, so keep a close eye on your pot!

CHOCOLATE-COCONUT RICE PUDDING

HANDS-ON: 5 MINUTES   TOTAL TIME: 20 MINUTES, PLUS COOLING
SERVES 8

1 Whisk together the coconut milk, whole milk, sugar, and salt in a medium saucepan over medium-high. Bring to a boil. Reduce heat to low, and simmer, stirring occasionally, until the mixture is reduced by half, about 15 minutes.

2 Meanwhile, heat another medium saucepan over medium-high. Add the shredded coconut, and cook, stirring often, until golden, 3 to 5 minutes. Remove from the heat.

3 When the coconut milk mixture has reduced by half, remove it from the heat; stir in the rice, chocolate chips, and vanilla. Cover and let the mixture steep for 10 minutes. Remove the lid and combine, making sure not to overmix. Cover and cool for 1 hour. Top each serving with toasted coconut.

1 (13 ½-ounce) can coconut milk

½ cup whole milk

½ cup sugar

½ teaspoon kosher salt

¾ cup sweetened shredded dried coconut

2 (10-ounce) pouches (about 2 cups) precooked brown rice microwaved according to package directions, cooled to room temperature

1 cup semisweet chocolate chips

1 teaspoon vanilla extract

CANNED TUNA

Canned tuna was a staple in our house when I was growing up. They were ten for a buck and my brother could turn them into a mean quesadilla with some Hormel chili— that's three food groups right there! I still love a can of tuna for the many quick and healthy dishes you can make with it.

I prefer to use canned tuna packed in water instead of oil. It's a little healthier and works better in my Universal Tuna Salad.

START WITH: UNIVERSAL TUNA SALAD

1 EZ BAKED TUNA ARANCINI
2 TUNA NIÇOISE BOATS
3 TUNA AND EGG DEMONS
4 TUNA PASTA SALAD
5 DECADENT CARAMELIZED TUNA PATTY MELTS

A very neutral base for all the recipes that follow, this tuna salad is dry enough to bake within a casserole, fry into arancini rice balls, or add to a salad bowl as is.

UNIVERSAL TUNA SALAD

HANDS-ON: 5 MINUTES   **TOTAL TIME:** 5 MINUTES   **MAKES** 1 ½ CUPS

1 Open the tuna cans and, using the back of a spoon, press as much of the liquid out as you can.

2 Whisk together the mayonnaise, lemon juice, olive oil, mustard, salt, and pepper in a small bowl. Fold in the tuna, and stir until incorporated.

3 (4-ounce) cans of tuna in water

1 tablespoon mayonnaise

1 tablespoon fresh lemon juice

1 teaspoon olive oil

½ teaspoon Dijon mustard

¼ teaspoon kosher salt

¼ teaspoon black pepper

1½ cups Universal Tuna Salad (page 193)

1½ cups microwaveable brown rice (from 10-ounce pouch), microwaved according to package directions

1½ cups panko (Japanese-style breadcrumbs)

¾ cup shredded mozzarella cheese (3 ounces)

½ cup firmly packed fresh basil leaves, chopped

½ cup firmly packed fresh flat-leaf parsley, chopped

½ cup whole milk

¼ cup freshly grated Parmesan cheese (1 ounce), plus more for serving

1 large egg, beaten

¾ teaspoon black pepper

½ teaspoon kosher salt

2 dashes of hot sauce, such as Tabasco

3 tablespoons extra-virgin olive oil

3 lemons, quartered

EXTRA CREDIT!

Serve with warm marinara sauce for dipping.

Arancini are Italian rice balls that are typically deep-fried. Baking them using quick and convenient microwaveable brown rice makes them a little healthier and a lot easier to prepare, with a lot less mess to clean up. A fun appetizer, these rice balls can go larger to serve as an entrée.

EZ BAKED TUNA ARANCINI

HANDS-ON: 10 MINUTES   TOTAL TIME: 30 MINUTES   SERVES 10

1 Preheat the oven to 425°F. Mix the tuna salad, rice, panko, mozzarella, basil, parsley, milk, Parmesan, egg, pepper, salt, hot sauce, and 1 tablespoon of the oil by hand in a large bowl until thoroughly combined.

2 Smear 1 tablespoon of the oil on a parchment paper–lined baking sheet. Using a small ice-cream scoop, spoon, or tablespoon, shape the tuna mixture into 40 balls (about 1 tablespoon each), and place them on the prepared baking sheet with the lemon wedges. Using a pastry brush, lightly brush the rice balls with the remaining 1 tablespoon oil. Bake until golden brown, 20 to 25 minutes. Squeeze the roasted lemons over the arancini, and top with the grated Parmesan.

2 / 8

1 ½ teaspoons kosher salt

24 fresh green beans, trimmed

12 ounces Yukon gold potatoes, cut into ½-inch-thick wedges

½ teaspoon dried oregano

12 tablespoons extra-virgin olive oil

1 teaspoon black pepper

3 tablespoons fresh lemon juice

1 tablespoon refrigerated garlic paste (from tube)

1 tablespoon water

1 head iceberg lettuce

12 cherry tomatoes, halved

1 ½ cups Universal Tuna Salad (page 193)

¾ cup diced cucumber

3 Foolproof Hard-Boiled Eggs (page 19), cut into quarters

3 tablespoons minced red onion

½ cup Kalamata olives, pitted and halved

One of my wife's favorite salads, this is a fun, family-style dish that allows you to do a little bit of showboating for your guests without much effort. Using lettuce leaves as the boat vessels keeps the presentation lighthearted, so you don't feel like a poser by making a salad you may not be able to pronounce. Say knee-soi-zzzz!

TUNA NIÇOISE BOATS

HANDS-ON: 20 MINUTES   TOTAL TIME: 45 MINUTES   SERVES 6

1 Bring 3 cups water and ½ teaspoon of the salt to a boil in a stockpot over high. Submerge the beans, and boil for 1 minute. Remove the beans with a slotted spoon, reserving the water in the stockpot. Plunge the beans into a bowl of ice water to stop the cooking process. Drain and pat them dry with paper towels. Cut in half lengthwise.

2 Add the potato wedges to the stockpot, and boil them until fork-tender, about 15 minutes. Drain the potatoes, cut the wedges in half, and then put them in a medium bowl with the oregano, 2 tablespoons of the oil, and ½ teaspoon of the pepper. Toss to coat.

3 Heat 2 tablespoons of the oil in a medium skillet over high. Cook the potatoes in the skillet, cut sides down, until golden and crispy, 3 to 5 minutes. Add 1 teaspoon of the lemon juice, and toss to combine. Return the potatoes to the bowl.

4 Whisk together the garlic paste and remaining ½ cup oil, 2 tablespoons plus 2 teaspoons lemon juice, 1 tablespoon water, and the remaining 1 teaspoon salt and ½ teaspoon pepper in a small bowl.

5 Cut the head of lettuce in half; remove the outer leaves and discard the core. Cut the larger outer leaves in half to create 6 "boats" of three to four layers each. Reserve the remaining lettuce for another use.

6 Arrange the lettuce boats on a platter, and then layer each one with the beans, potatoes, tomatoes, tuna salad, cucumber, eggs, onion, and olives. Serve with the garlicky lemon dressing.

Flex your culinary muscle a bit with these little devils, which use canned tuna and Swiss cheese to take this finger food favorite up a notch. Bring a platter of these to a party instead of deviled eggs, and you'll look like a fancy-pants chef. They're similar to a classic tuna melt, using hard-boiled eggs as the vessel in place of bread (though I'll soon teach you how to make Decadent Caramelized Tuna Patty Melts, page 200).

TUNA AND EGG DEMONS

HANDS-ON: 10 MINUTES   TOTAL TIME: 15 MINUTES   MAKES 18

1 Stir together the tuna salad, chives, mayonnaise, parsley, and paprika in a medium bowl.

2 Preheat the broiler, arranging a rack 6 inches from the heat source. Remove the yolks from the eggs, and add them to the tuna mixture, stirring to incorporate. Cut 4 of the cheese slices into quarters, and cut the remaining ½ cheese slice in half (to make 18 pieces in all). Spoon 1 rounded tablespoon of the tuna mixture into each egg white half, and top with 1 piece of pickled jalapeño and 1 piece of cheese.

3 Lightly coat an aluminum foil–lined baking sheet with cooking spray. Arrange the filled egg halves on the baking sheet in 3 rows, about 1 inch apart. Broil until the cheese is browned and bubbly, about 5 minutes.

1 cup Universal Tuna Salad (page 193)

2 tablespoons finely chopped fresh chives

1 tablespoon mayonnaise

1 tablespoon finely chopped fresh flat-leaf parsley leaves

½ teaspoon paprika

9 Foolproof Hard-Boiled Eggs (page 19), halved lengthwise, rounded bases trimmed to create a level surface

4 ½ slices Swiss cheese

9 pickled jalapeño chile slices, halved

EXTRA CREDIT!

When preparing the Universal Tuna Salad, substitute canned chicken or crabmeat for the canned tuna.

Take this pasta salad to any outdoor function, whether a potluck picnic or barbecue. It looks like a typical dish found at every party, but trust me when I tell you that it will totally stand out!

TUNA PASTA SALAD

HANDS-ON: 10 MINUTES   TOTAL TIME: 26 MINUTES
SERVES 10 AS A SIDE DISH

1 Stir together the tuna salad and ¼ teaspoon each of the salt and black pepper in a small bowl.

2 Process the oil, vinegar, mustard, honey, hot sauce, 2 tablespoons water, 1 teaspoon of the salt, and the remaining ½ teaspoon black pepper in a food processor until the vinaigrette is emulsified.

3 Bring 3 quarts of water and the remaining 1 teaspoon salt to a boil in a large stockpot over high. Add the pasta, and cook until al dente, 13 to 16 minutes (or according to package directions). Drain the pasta, and transfer to a large bowl. Toss with 2 tablespoons of the vinaigrette.

4 Add the roasted peppers, basil, onion, capers, lemon juice, oregano, and 6 tablespoons of the vinaigrette to the pasta, and toss to combine. Gently fold in the tuna salad mixture until incorporated. Serve at room temperature or chilled, with the remaining dressing on the side.

Make sure the salad is kept at room temperature or cooler—and don't leave it out for more than 2 hours. And watch out for the sun!

1 ½ cups Universal Tuna Salad (page 193)

2 ¼ teaspoons kosher salt

¾ teaspoon black pepper

½ cup olive oil

¼ cup red wine vinegar

2 tablespoons Dijon mustard

2 teaspoons honey

½ teaspoon hot sauce, such as Tabasco

2 tablespoons water

1 (12-ounce) package farfalle (bow-tie) pasta

1 cup jarred fire-roasted red bell peppers, sliced

1 cup firmly packed fresh basil leaves, cut into thin ribbons

½ cup diced red onion

2 tablespoons brined capers, drained and chopped

2 tablespoons fresh lemon juice

½ teaspoon dried oregano

5

My parents owned a fifties-style diner called Chubby's when I was a kid, so a patty melt was my introduction to rye bread. When I was studying for my baking degree, one of my favorite things to make was rye bread. If you don't yet appreciate the amazing flavor of caraway seed, it's one of those things that will sneak up on you and make you fall in love with it sooner or later.

DECADENT CARAMELIZED TUNA PATTY MELTS

HANDS-ON: 15 MINUTES   TOTAL TIME: 25 MINUTES   SERVES 4

THOUSAND ISLAND DRESSING

1 cup mayonnaise

¼ cup jarred pepperoncini peppers, drained, stems removed, finely chopped

¼ cup brined capers, drained and finely chopped

¼ cup finely chopped red onion

9 dill pickle chips, finely chopped

1 tablespoon plus 1 teaspoon ketchup

1 tablespoon fresh lemon juice

¼ teaspoon kosher salt

¼ teaspoon black pepper

1 ½ cups Universal Tuna Salad (page 193)

1 cup sauerkraut, drained and pressed dry

1 tablespoon vegetable oil

8 slices Russian rye bread

3 ounces (⅓ cup) unsalted butter, softened

8 slices Swiss cheese

1 Prepare the dressing: Stir together all the ingredients in a small bowl until well combined. Set aside.

2 Stir together the tuna salad and sauerkraut in a medium bowl, and divide the mixture into 4 equal portions. Using your hands, form each portion into a ball, and squeeze out any remaining liquid.

3 Heat the oil in a medium skillet over medium-high. Add the balls of tuna, pressing them into flat patties using a spatula. (It's okay if they run into each other.) Cook until caramelized on the bottom, 4 to 5 minutes. Gently turn the patties over, and cook until the other side is caramelized. Transfer the patties to a plate, and cover with aluminum foil to keep warm.

4 Spread 2 slices of the bread with ½ teaspoon butter on each side, and put them in the skillet over medium-low. Top each bread slice with a Swiss cheese slice, and cook until the cheese melts, about 1 minute. Spread 1 tablespoon of the dressing on each cheese slice. Top each with a warm tuna patty and 1 Swiss cheese slice. Top each sandwich with another slice of bread, and butter the outside of each bread slice with ½ teaspoon butter. Cook for 1 minute; turn and cook until the bread is toasted and the cheese is melted, another 1 to 2 minutes. Repeat the process to make 6 more patty melt sandwiches. Serve the sandwiches hot with the remaining dressing.

EXTRA CREDIT!

Serve the extra Thousand Island Dressing on the side to dip the sandwiches into, or squeeze a swipe of Sriracha chili sauce down the middle of each sandwich.

BREAD

Extra bread always gets wasted, and after seeing so many unused ends in the restaurant business I started thinking outside the stuffing box. My goal with this section is to show you how bread is not just a filler, it's a star! These smart recipes let you use leftover bread in brand-new ways. If your bread is going stale faster than you would like, or if you already have some partial loaves of bread stowed away in the freezer—there's now no excuse to throw them away!

LESS-FRESH BREAD

So, what can you do with less-than-fresh bread? You can make your own breadcrumbs by combining 8 cups of leftover bread in a food processor with 1 tablespoon each dried parsley, ranch dressing mix, dried minced onion, and dried oregano, and 1 teaspoon each garlic powder, salt, and pepper. You can also use extra chunks of old bread in any of the following dishes.

START WITH: LEFTOVER BREAD

1 CARAMELIZED ONION, CHIVE, AND MOZZARELLA MINI STRATAS
2 BY MISTAKE GARLIC BREAD SOUP
3 SAVORY BUTTERNUT SQUASH, KALE, AND MUSHROOM STUFFING
4 MATZO BALL SOUP
5 CREAM CHEESE CUSTARD FRENCH TOAST CASSEROLE

A strata is typically served as a layered casserole dish. Mine are miniature and easy to pop in your mouth, which can be dangerous when they disappear faster than you might expect! Each bite gives you a bit of irresistibly crunchy bread, fluffy eggs, and gooey cheese. Is it breakfast time yet?

6 large eggs

1 cup whole milk

1 cup shredded mozzarella cheese (4 ounces)

1 cup chopped fresh chives

½ cup heavy cream

1 tablespoon Dijon mustard

2 teaspoons kosher salt

1 teaspoon black pepper

2 dashes of hot sauce, such as Tabasco

¼ cup vegetable oil

2 cups diced yellow onion

2 tablespoons refrigerated garlic paste (from tube)

5 cups cubed leftover bread

CARAMELIZED ONION, CHIVE, AND MOZZARELLA MINI STRATAS

HANDS-ON: 25 MINUTES   TOTAL TIME: 55 MINUTES   SERVES 5

1 Preheat the oven to 400°F. Whisk together the eggs, milk, mozzarella, chives, cream, mustard, salt, pepper, and hot sauce in a large bowl.

2 Heat the oil in a medium skillet over high. Add the onion and garlic paste, and cook until the onions are well caramelized, 12 to 14 minutes. Add the onion mixture to the egg mixture in the bowl, and stir to combine. Let stand for 5 minutes.

3 Lightly grease 10 cups in a 12-cup muffin pan with nonstick cooking spray. Scoop ½ cup of the bread cubes into each greased muffin cup. Top each with ½ cup of the egg mixture, stirring gently to combine. Try to lift up the mixture while scooting in the excess from the sides. (You may make a mess, but the strata tops likely will run together in the oven anyway, so it is fine.)

4 Put the muffin pan on an aluminum foil–lined baking sheet. Bake until golden brown, about 30 minutes. Serve warm.

The bigger and more jagged your bread pieces are, the better for holding flavor.

½ cup vegetable oil

4 cups roughly chopped yellow onion

1 cup roughly chopped celery

2 bay leaves

2 tablespoons garlic powder

1 tablespoon garlic salt

1 cup refrigerated garlic paste
(from tube)

1 cup white wine

4 cups cubed or torn leftover bread

6 cups chicken stock

1 cup heavy cream

Chopped fresh flat leaf Italian parsley,
for garnish

Sour cream, for serving

When I cooked at the now-defunct Myth Cafe in San Francisco, I was known for my soups, and customers began to expect me to come up with two to three new ones each day. Eventually, it was getting to that point where I was running out of ideas, but the one thing I always had was stale ends of bread. An early version of this soup was essentially created by mistake, but it was so popular it stayed on the menu for a long time.

BY MISTAKE GARLIC BREAD SOUP

HANDS-ON: 10 MINUTES   TOTAL TIME: 20 MINUTES
MAKES 8 TO 10 CUPS

Combine the oil, onion, celery, bay leaves, garlic powder, garlic salt, and garlic paste in a medium Dutch oven over medium heat, and cook until soft, about 10 minutes. Add the white wine, and reduce the heat to a simmer. Add the bread, chicken stock, and cream, and simmer for 10 minutes. Remove and discard the bay leaves. Puree in a blender. Garnish with the chopped parsley, and serve with the sour cream.

People think of stuffing as a side you only enjoy once a year, but it can be great to serve it year round. This version skips the festive Thanksgiving combo of sage, parsley, and thyme and uses hearty ingredients like kale, mushrooms, and scallions for a hit that transcends the holiday season.

SAVORY BUTTERNUT SQUASH, KALE, AND MUSHROOM STUFFING

HANDS-ON: 20 MINUTES **TOTAL TIME: 1 HOUR 5 MINUTES**
SERVES 12 AS A SIDE DISH

1 Preheat the oven to 400°F. Combine the bread and milk in a 13- x 9-inch baking dish; let stand for 15 minutes.

2 Meanwhile, combine the onion, mushrooms, oil, salt, pepper, and chile flakes in a Dutch oven or large heavy-bottomed pot over high. Cook until the mushrooms are tender, about 10 minutes. Add the kale, squash, and scallions; cook until the kale is wilted, 2 to 3 minutes. Remove from the heat; stir in the stock and lemon juice. Add the bread mixture, and stir to combine. Stir in the eggs.

3 Wipe the 13- x 9-inch baking dish clean, and lightly coat it with nonstick cooking spray. Transfer the stuffing mixture to the prepared baking dish. Bake, uncovered, for 45 minutes. Increase the heat to broil, and broil until the top is browned and bubbly, about 2 minutes.

12 cups cubed or torn leftover bread

1 cup whole milk

3 cups diced yellow onion

2 cups sliced cremini mushrooms

½ cup vegetable oil

1 tablespoon kosher salt

1 teaspoon black pepper

⅛ teaspoon red chile flakes

6 cups chopped kale leaves

1 (10-ounce) package frozen cubed raw butternut squash

1 cup scallions, chopped

1 cup chicken or vegetable stock

1 tablespoon fresh lemon juice

2 large eggs, beaten

This simple soother is reminiscent of the Jewish comfort classic, matzo ball soup. Lesley and I love the dumplings even more than the soup, so when we make this together, we always poach extra dumplings on the side so they're ready to toss into the soup.

MATZO BALL SOUP

HANDS-ON: 35 MINUTES   TOTAL TIME: 1 HOUR   SERVES 6

1 Combine the bread and milk in a microwave-safe dish; microwave on High for 1 minute 30 seconds; let stand for 10 minutes. Stir in the parsley, eggs, garlic paste, pepper, and 2 teaspoons of the salt. Stir in the flour, and set aside.

2 Combine the onion, celery, carrot, oil, bay leaves, and remaining 1 teaspoon salt in a Dutch oven or large heavy-bottomed pot over medium-high. Cover and cook, stirring often, until the vegetables are softened, about 10 minutes. Add the chicken stock, shredded chicken, and 2 cups water; bring to a boil.

3 Using wet hands, form the bread mixture into 12 golf ball–sized dumplings. Carefully ease the dumplings into the soup. Cover and reduce the heat to medium-low. Simmer until the dumplings float, about 10 minutes. Remove from the heat; let stand, covered, for 10 minutes before serving. Remove and discard the bay leaves.

4 cups cubed or torn leftover bread

1 cup whole milk

½ cup loosely packed chopped fresh flat-leaf parsley

2 large eggs, beaten

1 tablespoon refrigerated garlic paste (from tube)

1 teaspoon black pepper

3 teaspoons kosher salt

¾ cup all-purpose flour

2 cups diced yellow onion

1 cup diced celery

1 cup diced carrot

¼ cup vegetable oil

2 bay leaves

6 cups chicken stock

4 cups shredded cooked chicken

2 cups water

1 ½ cups heavy cream

8 ounces cream cheese, softened (about 1 cup)

4 large eggs

3 large egg yolks

1 ½ cups whole milk

¼ cup granulated sugar

1 ½ tablespoons vanilla extract

⅛ teaspoon ground nutmeg

½ cup maple syrup

1 ¼ teaspoons kosher salt

6 cups cubed or torn leftover bread

1 (16-ounce) package frozen strawberries

¼ cup water

Confectioners' sugar, for dusting

I love making French toast for guests, but it can be a pain if you have to make too many individual portions. The solution is this decadent casserole that feeds everyone all at the same time —no dipping and flipping slices one at a time required.

CREAM CHEESE CUSTARD FRENCH TOAST CASSEROLE

HANDS-ON: 35 MINUTES   TOTAL: 2 HOURS   SERVES 8

1 Process the cream, cream cheese, eggs, and egg yolks in a blender until smooth. Transfer the mixture to a large bowl. Add the milk, granulated sugar, vanilla extract, nutmeg, ¼ cup of the maple syrup, and 1 teaspoon of the salt; stir until smooth. Add the bread, and stir until fully incorporated. Chill for 30 minutes, stirring after 15 minutes.

2 Preheat the oven to 400°F. Combine the strawberries, ¼ cup water, the remaining ¼ cup maple syrup, and the remaining ¼ teaspoon salt in a medium saucepan over medium-high. Bring to a boil; reduce the heat to low and simmer, mashing the strawberries often with a potato masher, until they are fully cooked and completely broken down, about 5 minutes. Cook a little longer if you want a thicker sauce. Remove from the heat.

3 Transfer the chilled bread mixture to a 9-inch square baking dish, and mash it down with a spoon or spatula. It may seem soupy, but that's what you want. Cover the dish with aluminum foil.

4 Put the casserole dish inside a large roasting pan with high sides, and put the roasting pan in the preheated oven. Fill the roasting pan with boiling water halfway up the sides of the casserole dish. Bake until a wooden pick or toothpick inserted in the center comes out clean, about 1 hour. If there is still too much liquid, bake an additional 10 minutes.

5 Heat the strawberry sauce over low just until warmed through. Dust the casserole with the confectioners' sugar, and serve the French toast with the warm strawberry sauce.

CANNED CHICKPEAS

Until quinoa became popular I would have called chickpeas the most balanced vegetarian protein, but damn you, quinoa! I still love 'em even though they're second place—they're a super-cheap and flexible ingredient that doesn't have to be the front-runner, but is always in the game. Canned chickpeas are easy to find in the grocery store where you might also see them labeled as garbanzo beans. All you need to do is open up the can, rinse, and drain them. Now, you're good to go!

EXTRA CREDIT!

Revive the crunch the next day
by reheating the chickpeas for
5 minutes at 500°F.

Talk about a crowd-pleaser! I love lemon and heat together, and here I've incorporated both into a snack that doesn't bust the waistline. It's ideal as an appetizer as well as a salad topper, or a juxtaposition to vegetable dishes.

LEMONY BAKED CHICKPEAS

HANDS-ON: 10 MINUTES   TOTAL TIME: 35 MINUTES   SERVES 6

Preheat the oven to 450°F. Combine the olive oil, lemon zest, cumin, salt, black pepper, oregano, chili powder, and chile flakes in a medium bowl, and stir until a nice paste forms. Toss in the chickpeas, and stir until evenly coated. Spread the chickpeas in an even layer on an aluminum foil–lined rimmed baking sheet, and bake until browned and crunchy, 25 to 30 minutes, shaking the pan occasionally.

1 tablespoon extra-virgin olive oil

1 tablespoon lemon zest

1 teaspoon ground cumin

1 teaspoon kosher salt

½ teaspoon black pepper

½ teaspoon dried oregano

½ teaspoon chili powder

¼ teaspoon red chile flakes

2 (16-ounce) cans chickpeas, drained and patted dry with a paper towel

2

One of my mentors, Gary Danko, showed me that simple, salty, and delicious ingredients can dress up any salad. This is a homage to him that's reminiscent of a version he used to do when I worked for him. It's vibrant, has a zesty pop, and is super easy to make. People definitely ask for this one a lot!

CHICKPEA, CAPER, AND RED ONION VINAIGRETTE

HANDS-ON: 10 MINUTES   **TOTAL TIME: 10 MINUTES**   **SERVES 12**

½ cup red wine vinegar

2 teaspoons refrigerated garlic paste (from tube)

¼ cup Dijon mustard

¼ cup minced red onion

2 tablespoons brined capers, drained and minced

½ teaspoon sugar

2 teaspoons kosher salt

1 teaspoon black pepper

2 tablespoons finely chopped fresh flat-leaf parsley

1 ¼ cups extra-virgin olive oil

1 (16-ounce) can chickpeas, drained

Combine the vinegar, garlic paste, mustard, onions, capers, sugar, salt, and pepper in a medium bowl, and let sit for 5 minutes to break down the rawness of the red onion. Add the parsley, olive oil, and chickpeas, and stir until incorporated.

This will keep in the fridge for a few days, but only add the parsley to what you're serving that day. Otherwise the herbs will oxidize from the vinegar.

EXTRA CREDIT!

This is great over chicken, shrimp, or fish. One of my favorites is serving this on top of lightly-steamed asparagus.

EXTRA CREDIT!
Top with Lemony Baked
Chickpeas (page 215).

This is a play on spinach dip without the spinach, because I can't just show up at a party with ho-hum spinach dip. You may have noticed that I love ranch dressing and feta cheese; this combo creates a really killer dip that will make everyone at the party happy.

CHICKPEA, ASPARAGUS, AND FETA DIP

HANDS-ON: 10 MINUTES   TOTAL TIME: 40 MINUTES
SERVES 8 TO 10 AS AN APPETIZER

1 Preheat the oven to 400°F. Process the cream cheese, sour cream, lemon juice, ranch dressing mix, and pepper in a food processor until smooth.

2 Heat the oil in a large skillet over high. Add the onion, and cook, stirring constantly, until caramelized, about 2 minutes. Add the asparagus and garlic paste, and cook, stirring constantly, until done, about 3 minutes. Remove from the heat.

3 Spoon the cream cheese mixture into a medium bowl. Add the scallions, feta, chickpeas, and onion-asparagus mixture, and stir together until incorporated. Spoon the dip mixture into a 9-inch deep-dish pie pan or baking dish.

4 Stir together the breadcrumbs and melted butter, and spread over the dip. Bake until the top is gooey and bubbly, 25 to 30 minutes. Serve with slices or torn pieces of baguette.

2 (8-ounce) packages cream cheese, softened

2 tablespoons sour cream

2 tablespoons fresh lemon juice

3 teaspoons ranch dressing mix, such as Hidden Valley

1 teaspoon black pepper

¼ cup vegetable oil

1 cup diced yellow onion

2 cups chopped fresh asparagus (about ¼-inch pieces)

1 teaspoon refrigerated garlic paste (from tube)

1 cup chopped scallions

6 ounces crumbled feta cheese (1½ cups)

1 (16-ounce) can chickpeas, drained

½ cup panko (Japanese-style breadcrumbs)

1 tablespoon salted butter, melted

1 baguette, sliced or torn

4

1 (16-ounce) can chickpeas, drained

¼ cup plain fat-free Greek yogurt

¼ cup mayonnaise

¼ cup sour cream

1 teaspoon whole-grain mustard

1 tablespoon fresh lemon juice

3 dashes of hot sauce, such as Tabasco

1 teaspoon sugar

½ teaspoon red chile flakes

½ teaspoon kosher salt

½ teaspoon black pepper

½ cup diced Bosc pear

½ cup red seedless grapes, halved or quartered

¼ cup diced red onion

½ cup diced celery

¼ cup loosely packed fresh flat-leaf parsley, chopped

½ cup toasted walnuts, chopped

3 cups firmly packed fresh spinach leaves

Some of my most vivid culinary memories are of my grandmother Lena, who would let me mess up every meal she made. She was the only person I knew who could drop half of her meal on her dress and say, "Don't worry about it honey, I'm saving it for later!" (Miss you!) Her Waldorf salad was really popular during the holiday seasons. Mine has pears and includes fat-free Greek yogurt and sour cream in addition to the mayonnaise that she used exclusively in her version.

LENA'S CHICKPEA–PEAR WALDORF SALAD

HANDS-ON: 10 MINUTES   TOTAL TIME: 10 MINUTES, PLUS CHILLING
SERVES 6

Stir together the chickpeas, yogurt, mayonnaise, sour cream, mustard, lemon juice, hot sauce, sugar, chile flakes, salt, and black pepper in a medium bowl. Add the pears, grapes, onion, celery, parsley, and walnuts, and stir until incorporated. Fold in the spinach, and refrigerate for 1 hour before serving.

I travel a lot and one of my favorite places to go is London, which has an unbelievable amount of great Indian food. This is my take on a popular Indian dish called *chana masala* that utilizes familiar and perhaps unexpected spices from your cabinet.

PEASANT BEANS WITH CUCUMBER SALAD

HANDS-ON: 10 MINUTES   TOTAL TIME: 15 MINUTES   SERVES 8

1 Prepare the salad: If you're shredding the cucumber yourself in a food processor (rather than buying it preshredded), squeeze out the liquid. Toss together the cucumber, yogurt, lemon juice, salt, and pepper in a bowl. Set aside.

2 Prepare the beans: Process the onion, tomatoes, jalapeño, ginger paste, garlic paste, and chili paste in a food processor until it looks like a salsa, about 10 seconds.

3 Stir together the coriander, pumpkin pie spice, salt, chili powder, onion powder, paprika, and cumin in a small bowl.

4 Heat the oil in a stockpot or Dutch oven over high. Add the bay leaves, and cook, stirring constantly, until fragrant and brown, about 10 to 15 seconds. Add the onion-tomato mixture, and cook, stirring occasionally, until the mixture is thickened and looks almost like a gravy with both oily and tomato parts, about 5 minutes. Stir in the spice mixture, and cook for 2 more minutes. Add the chickpeas, and reduce the heat to medium-low. Simmer for 5 minutes. Discard the bay leaves. Spoon over bowls of brown rice, and garnish with chopped fresh cilantro. Serve with the cucumber salad.

2 cups shredded English cucumber

¾ cup plain whole-milk Greek yogurt

1 tablespoon fresh lemon juice

1 teaspoon kosher salt

¼ teaspoon black pepper

2 cups diced yellow or white onion

2 cups diced plum tomatoes

3 tablespoons seeded chopped jalapeño chile

2 tablespoons refrigerated ginger paste (from tube)

2 tablespoons refrigerated garlic paste (from tube)

1 tablespoon refrigerated chili paste (from tube)

1 teaspoon ground coriander

1 teaspoon pumpkin pie spice

1 teaspoon kosher salt

1 teaspoon chili powder

1 teaspoon onion powder

½ teaspoon paprika

1 teaspoon ground cumin

¼ cup vegetable oil

2 bay leaves

2 (16-ounce) cans chickpeas, drained

2 (8.5-ounce) pouches microwaveable brown rice, cooked

½ cup loosely packed fresh cilantro, chopped

CHOCOLATE

A lot of people don't know that I went to pastry school, where I learned how to make chocolate ganache, an incredible building block for so many desserts. My goal for this book is to give you an arsenal of skills without a $45,000 tuition price tag, and one of my top tips would be to learn how to make this super-easy and amazingly universal treat. Using my basic ganache recipe, you can frost a cake or cupcake or whip up any of my other one-to-five desserts.

START WITH: RYAN'S QUICK CHOCOLATE GANACHE

1 ROCKY ROAD FUDGE
2 SWEET AND SALTY CHOCOLATE BARK
3 CHOCOLATE CONFETTI TRUFFLES
4 BAILEYS CHOCOLATE MOUSSE
5 MAMA PAT'S CHOCOLATE BROWNIE PIE

Ganache is basically a fancy way to say chocolate and cream, and it doesn't take fancy technique to make it. Refrigerate your ganache if you plan to make Chocolate Confetti Truffles (page 231), or let sit out for 20 or 30 minutes if you're making Baileys Chocolate Mousse (page 233) or the other three recipes.

RYAN'S QUICK CHOCOLATE GANACHE

HANDS-ON: 5 MINUTES   TOTAL TIME: 15 MINUTES   MAKES 2 CUPS

2 ½ cups semisweet chocolate chips

1 cup heavy cream

1 tablespoon light corn syrup

1 teaspoon vanilla extract

⅛ teaspoon kosher salt

1 Put the chocolate chips in a heatproof mixing bowl. Stir together the cream, corn syrup, vanilla, and salt in a small saucepan; bring to a boil over medium-high. Pour the hot cream mixture over the chocolate chips, making sure all the chips are submerged. (Do not stir or touch the chocolate mixture.) Cover the bowl with plastic wrap, and let it stand for 5 minutes.

2 Using a spatula and starting from the bottom of the bowl, gently move the mixture from side to side to begin combining the chocolate with the cream mixture. Gradually and slowly stir from the middle until smooth and blended, 2 to 3 minutes.

If you get granules while making your ganache, pop the bowl in the microwave for 10 seconds and keep going!

The ganache is best when you use it right away, but if you do need to make it ahead, reheat it in the microwave on Medium, for 15-second intervals, stirring gently, until it returns to the correct consistency.

1

Ryan's Quick Chocolate Ganache (page 227)

Nonstick cooking spray

1 cup miniature marshmallows

1 cup toasted walnut halves

⅛ teaspoon cayenne pepper

A love child of fudge and rocky road ice cream (with a little kick of cayenne), this treat couldn't be quicker to make. The only problem is that it will test your patience as you wait for it to chill in the fridge. Trust me, though, it's worth the wait!

ROCKY ROAD FUDGE

HANDS-ON: 5 MINUTES   TOTAL TIME: 20 MINUTES, PLUS CHILLING
MAKES 64 SQUARES

1 Let the prepared ganache stand at room temperature until slightly cooled, about 20 minutes. (The ganache should be smooth and spreadable.) Line an 8-inch square cake pan with heavy-duty aluminum foil, allowing 2 to 3 inches to extend over the sides; coat the foil with nonstick cooking spray.

2 Toss together the marshmallows, walnuts, and cayenne; using a spatula, spread half of the mixture on the bottom of the prepared pan. Spread 1 cup ganache over the top. Repeat the layers once; coat the top with cooking spray. Cover with plastic wrap, gently pressing the plastic wrap directly on the fudge. Chill in the refrigerator for 4 hours.

3 When the fudge is thoroughly chilled, remove the plastic wrap. Lift the fudge from the pan using the foil sides as handles. Invert the fudge onto a cutting board; carefully remove the foil. Using a warm, slightly wet knife, cut the fudge into squares or triangles. (Wipe the knife blade with a warm, wet cloth in between cuts to maintain clean edges on the cut sides of the fudge pieces.)

2

I like to think of this bark as an adult version of a Twix bar. You can't beat peanuts and pretzels for nostalgic crunch, and the sesame seeds offer a sophisticated twist.

SWEET AND SALTY CHOCOLATE BARK

HANDS-ON: 15 MINUTES   TOTAL TIME: 15 MINUTES, PLUS CHILLING
MAKES ABOUT 2 POUNDS

2 cups semisweet chocolate chips

Ryan's Quick Chocolate Ganache (page 227)

2 cups pretzel sticks

1 cup dry-roasted peanuts

2 tablespoons sesame seeds

1 Line a rimmed baking sheet with parchment paper; coat the parchment with nonstick cooking spray.

2 Microwave the semisweet chocolate chips in a microwave-safe bowl on High until melted and smooth, about 2 minutes, stirring every 15 seconds. Slowly pour the melted chocolate into the prepared pan, spreading it into a thin (about ⅛-inch), even layer. Chill until firm, about 30 minutes.

3 Meanwhile, let the prepared ganache stand at room temperature until slightly cooled, about 20 minutes. (The ganache should be smooth and spreadable.)

4 Using a spatula, spread the ganache evenly over the hardened chocolate layer in the pan. Sprinkle the pretzel sticks, peanuts, and sesame seeds evenly over the top, gently pressing them into the ganache to adhere. Chill the bark until firm, about 2 hours. Cut or break into pieces.

Truffles sound like an intimidating challenge for advanced chefs only, but this festive take on this confection is by far the easiest recipe in the whole chapter. Shh—you don't have to tell your guests! ☺

CHOCOLATE CONFETTI TRUFFLES

HANDS-ON: 15 MINUTES   TOTAL TIME: 15 MINUTES, PLUS CHILLING
MAKES 40

Using your hands, shape the chilled ganache into 40 balls (about ½ tablespoon each). Roll 20 balls in the confectioners' sugar and the remaining 20 balls in the candy sprinkles, and place them on parchment paper-lined baking sheets. Chill for 2 hours.

Ryan's Quick Chocolate Ganache (page 227), chilled for 4 hours

½ cup confectioners' sugar

½ cup rainbow candy sprinkles

EXTRA CREDIT!

Serve family style in one bowl
with a topping bar that includes
toasted coconut, nuts, fruit,
chocolate chips, grated chocolate
or chocolate curls.

A shot of Baileys makes my rich chocolate mousse a little bit naughty—and one you won't soon forget. If you want to get even crazier, you can substitute a shot of espresso or Fireball cinnamon whisky!

BAILEYS CHOCOLATE MOUSSE

HANDS-ON: 15 MINUTES   TOTAL TIME: 55 MINUTES   SERVES 8

1 Let the ganache stand at room temperature for 30 minutes.

2 Put the heavy cream in the bowl of a stand mixer fitted with a whisk attachment. (If desired, cover the mixer with a large clean towel to avoid splatters.) Beat the cream at medium-high speed until medium peaks form, about 4 minutes. (You can remove the whisk attachment and dip it into the whipped cream to test the peaks.)

3 Beat one-third of the whipped cream into the cooled ganache using an electric mixer at medium speed. Stir in the liqueur. Using a spatula, fold in the remaining whipped cream by slicing or cutting down through the middle of the ganache mixture and folding in more whipped cream while turning the bowl. Repeat the procedure (which helps to aerate the mousse) until the ganache and whipped cream are completely incorporated. Serve immediately or cover and refrigerate for up to 2 days.

Ryan's Quick Chocolate Ganache (page 227)

3 cups heavy cream

2 tablespoons Irish cream liqueur, such as Baileys

5

1 (9-inch) frozen unbaked piecrust shell

Ryan's Quick Chocolate Ganache
  (page 227)

1 cup store-bought brownies, cut into
  ½-inch cubes (2 to 3 brownies)

½ cup store-bought caramel sauce

1 cup heavy cream

2 teaspoons instant espresso

Confectioners' sugar, for dusting

I think my mom was the first Sandra Lee way before semi-homemade was Semi-Homemade. Thanks to easy dessert ideas like this, we always had something to serve when neighbors just dropped in for a visit.

MAMA PAT'S CHOCOLATE BROWNIE PIE

HANDS-ON: 15 MINUTES   **TOTAL TIME: 1 HOUR, PLUS CHILLING**
SERVES 8

1 Preheat the oven to 375°F. Line the piecrust shell with parchment paper, and fill it with pie weights, dried beans, or uncooked rice. Bake for 15 minutes. Remove the pie weights and parchment paper. Return the piecrust to the oven, and bake until lightly browned, about 5 minutes more. Remove to a wire rack, and cool for 30 minutes.

2 Meanwhile, let the prepared ganache stand at room temperature 30 minutes.

3 Sprinkle the brownie cubes on the bottom of the piecrust; top with the caramel sauce, drizzling it evenly. Beat the ganache, heavy cream, and espresso with an electric mixer on medium-high speed until fluffy. Using a spatula, spread the ganache mixture evenly over the top of the pie.

4 Chill the pie, uncovered, for 2 hours. Dust with the confectioners' sugar just before serving.

CAKE MIX

Forget the instructions that are printed on your cake mix package—this is your time to bake outside the box! You don't have to spend time sifting ingredients together and making a mess in order to make delicious churros, waffles, bars, cookies, and streusel. My cake mix of choice is Pillsbury Moist Supreme Classic White, but you should feel free to pick your favorite brand to use with these recipes. You won't have to do anything besides open the box to get started.

AS ALWAYS,
PUDDING IN THE

Waffles are near and dear to me because I used to work at a place (still owned by my good buddy David Duncan) called Country Waffles with my mom when I was in junior high and high school—it was like the Central Californian version of Waffle House. I always keep Key lime juice in my fridge now to make these citrus-spiked beauties. This is a breakfast must.

KEY LIME-AND-RASPBERRY WAFFLES

HANDS-ON: 20 MINUTES   TOTAL TIME: 25 MINUTES   SERVES 4

1 Stir together the cake mix, cornstarch, baking soda, and salt in a mixing bowl. Add the oil, eggs, lime juice, vanilla, lime zest, and ½ cup water; stir until fully incorporated.

2 Lightly grease a waffle iron with nonstick cooking spray, and heat according to the manufacturer's instructions. Pour the batter into the waffle iron squares until two-thirds full. Place 2 to 3 raspberries on each waffle, and add a little more batter to cover the raspberries. Close the lid, and cook until the waffles are browned, 4 to 5 minutes. Transfer the waffles to a plate, and repeat the procedure until you've used all the batter.

3 Serve the hot waffles with the remaining raspberries and maple syrup.

1 box white cake mix, such as Pillsbury Moist Supreme Classic White

½ cup cornstarch

1 teaspoon baking soda

1 teaspoon kosher salt

½ cup vegetable oil

2 large eggs

¼ cup bottled Key lime juice

1 tablespoon vanilla extract

1 tablespoon lime zest

½ cup water

1 cup fresh raspberries

Maple syrup, for serving

2

STREUSEL (makes about 7 cups)

1 box white cake mix, such as Pillsbury Moist Supreme Classic White

½ cup firmly packed light or dark brown sugar

8 ounces (1 cup) unsalted butter, chilled and cut into cubes

2 large eggs

1 cup all-purpose flour

¼ cup vegetable oil

SHAKES

2 tablespoons vegetable oil

3 bananas, sliced

1 cup caramel-flavored ice-cream topping

¼ cup heavy cream

10 ½ cups vanilla ice cream

2 cups Cake Streusel, plus more for serving

1 ½ cups whole milk

¾ teaspoon kosher salt

Quick! Make this and tell me it isn't the most delicious, over-the-top milkshake you've ever had! You'll have a decent amount of leftover cake streusel, which you'll be happy about because it's the perfect decadent little topping for fruit and yogurt.

BANANAS FOSTER SHAKES WITH CAKE STREUSEL

HANDS-ON: 45 MINUTES   TOTAL TIME: 1 HOUR 50 MINUTES   SERVES 6

1 Prepare the streusel: Preheat the oven to 375°F. Beat the cake mix and brown sugar on low speed in the bowl of a stand mixer until combined, about 1 minute. Add the butter, and beat until the mixture starts to crumble, 30 to 45 seconds. (It's okay to have some small pieces and some large, or if the mixture is wet in one spot and dry in another.) Add the eggs, and beat until incorporated, about 1 minute. Add the flour and vegetable oil, and beat just until incorporated, 5 to 10 seconds. (Do not overmix.)

2 Lightly grease an aluminum foil–lined rimmed baking sheet with nonstick cooking spray. Spread the streusel mixture out on the prepared baking sheet, and flatten it with a spatula. (Don't worry if it has some peaks and valleys.) Bake, stirring every 10 to 15 minutes, until browned and crumbly, 35 to 40 minutes total. Transfer the baking sheet to a wire rack, and let the streusel cool completely, about 20 minutes.

3 When the streusel is cooked, prepare the shakes: Heat the vegetable oil in a medium saucepan over medium-high. Add the banana slices to the hot oil, and cook until softened and just beginning to brown, about 5 minutes. Drain the oil from the saucepan. Add the caramel topping and cream to the bananas, and bring to a boil over medium. Cook, stirring often, until the bananas are caramelized, about 3 minutes.

4 For each shake, process 1 ¾ cups ice cream, ⅓ cup cake streusel, ¼ cup milk, ⅛ teaspoon salt, and one-sixth of the banana mixture in a blender until smooth, 10 to 20 seconds. Pour into a tall glass, and top with a sprinkle of cake streusel. Serve immediately.

These deep-fried treats are a big hit at Market & Rye, where they're served with a chocolate-coffee dipping sauce. This pumpkin-flavored rendition is a welcome addition to the table at any time of year.

PUMPKIN CHURROS

HANDS-ON: 10 MINUTES **TOTAL TIME: 20 MINUTES** **MAKES 30 TO 40**

4 cups vegetable oil

1 box white cake mix, such as Pillsbury Moist Supreme Classic White

1 (15-ounce) can pumpkin puree

1 cup all-purpose flour

2 large eggs

1 tablespoon vanilla extract

1 teaspoon kosher salt

⅛ teaspoon ground nutmeg

⅛ teaspoon ground cloves

2 tablespoons plus 1 teaspoon pumpkin pie spice

1 cup sugar

1 Heat the oil in a medium Dutch oven or other heavy-bottomed pot over medium-high until a deep-fry thermometer reaches 375°F.

2 Meanwhile, stir together the cake mix, pumpkin, flour, eggs, vanilla, salt, nutmeg, cloves, and 1 teaspoon of the pumpkin pie spice in a large mixing bowl. Transfer the dough to a large zip-top plastic freezer bag, and cut off one bottom corner to make a ½-inch hole (see Note).

3 Working in batches, pipe about 3-inch lengths of dough into the hot oil; use scissors or a knife to cut the dough between pieces. (It's okay if the churros curl into shapes.) Fry, turning occasionally, until the churros float in the oil and are golden brown on both sides, 2 to 3 minutes. Using a slotted spoon, remove the churros to a plate lined with paper towels to drain; blot the churros with more paper towels. Repeat with the remaining batter.

4 Stir together the sugar and remaining 2 tablespoons pumpkin pie spice in a shallow dish. Roll the churros in the sugar mixture to coat while they're still hot.

For prettier churros, use a pastry bag with a star tip.

EXTRA CREDIT!

Serve with caramel sauce for dipping or pair with a café au lait.

Who doesn't love a blondie? Mine includes all of my favorite candy bars in a single batch because more is better. If you're ever going to cheat on your diet, this is so worth it. But if you're offended by the splurge, I would like to direct you to my section on kale (page 76).

1 box white cake mix, such as Pillsbury Moist Supreme Classic White

3 large eggs

½ cup vegetable oil

⅓ cup creamy peanut butter

½ teaspoon kosher salt

1 cup Milky Way Original Minis

1 cup Reese's Peanut Butter Cups Miniatures

1 cup Butterfinger Bites

HIDDEN SECRETS CANDY BAR BARS

HANDS-ON: 10 MINUTES   TOTAL TIME: 3 HOURS   MAKES 12

1 Preheat the oven to 350°F. Beat the cake mix, eggs, oil, peanut butter, and salt at low speed in the bowl of a stand mixer until incorporated, about 3 minutes. Add the candy, and beat until incorporated, about 30 seconds.

2 Line a 9- x 9-inch baking dish with heavy-duty aluminum foil, allowing 2 to 3 inches to extend over the sides; lightly grease the foil with nonstick cooking spray.

3 Spread the dough evenly in the prepared baking dish. Place a piece of parchment paper directly on the dough, pressing to flatten it. Spread dried rice or dried beans on the parchment to weigh down the dough. Bake, pressing down on the rice or beans with a spatula every 15 to 20 minutes, until a wooden pick inserted into the center of the bars comes out clean, 50 to 55 minutes total.

4 Transfer the baking dish to a wire rack, discard the parchment and rice or beans, and cool for 2 hours before cutting the bars into squares or triangles.

This is a cake mix version of the Kitchen Sink Cookies we make at Market & Rye. There, they are almost as big as your head, but here they're miniaturized, which should all but guarantee that they won't be around for long.

KITCHEN SINK COOKIES

HANDS-ON: 15 MINUTES   TOTAL TIME: 40 MINUTES   MAKES 36

1 Preheat the oven to 350°F. Line 2 baking sheets with parchment paper.

2 In a stand mixer, combine the cake mix, butter, eggs, vanilla extract, and salt, and mix until smooth, scraping down the sides of the bowl with a spatula as you go. Add the coconut, milk chocolate chips, semisweet chocolate chips, and white chocolate chips, and mix until well incorporated; add the pecans, pretzel sticks, and candy, and mix just until incorporated. You'll have big chunks of the add-ins sticking out of the dough, and that is okay.

3 Working in batches, use a large (2-tablespoon) cookie scoop to measure out balls of dough onto the prepared baking sheets. Press down on the balls of dough slightly with dampened fingers. Bake for 12 to 14 minutes. Let the cookies stand on the baking sheets for 2 minutes, and then remove them to wire racks to cool completely. Repeat with the remaining batter.

1 box white cake mix, such as Pillsbury Moist Supreme Classic White

8 ounces (1 cup) unsalted butter, at room temperature

2 large eggs

1 teaspoon vanilla extract

½ teaspoon salt

½ cup packed sweetened shredded coconut

½ cup milk chocolate chips

½ cup semisweet chocolate chips

½ cup white chocolate chips

½ cup toasted chopped pecans

1 cup broken pretzel sticks

¾ cup M&M's

ACKNOWLEDGMENTS

Boy, oh boy. How do you write acknowledgments for a list of people as long as a Danielle Steel novel? This book is the result of so many years of life, education, and plain, hard work. I'm sorry if I forget a few of the people who helped me in my journey, but I'm going to take a stab at it.

To Lesley, my amazingly supportive, beautiful wife, this world made sense when I met you, and this book is complete because of you. Thank you for your hard work and dedication and sleepless nights helping to write this. Because of you, this book is on shelves everywhere ☺. I love you so much BBB.

To Mom, the mold was broken when you came into this world. I owe you everything: who I am, who I've become, and who I will be. I truly, truly am the luckiest man in the world to call you Mom. Thank you for being you and thank you for loving us.

To Danny, boy you didn't know what you signed up for when you married my mom (meaning you got me as a stepson). You go above and beyond and I am the man I am today because of you. Thanks for loving us unconditionally because we love you unconditionally. There is no step in front of calling you Dad.

To my in-laws, Bonnie and Michael, I struck gold when I married your daughter and in having you two as family. Thank you for your support, thank you for allowing me to fall asleep anywhere and everywhere, and thank you for allowing me to step into your kitchen and help with the holiday meals. I love you both so much.

To David Duncan at Country Waffles in Los Baños, California, everything you taught me in my teens was right, and all the a$$ kicking you did truly set me up for my future. I love you, buddy.

To Steve Hernandez, "WHAT THE HELL ARE YOU DOING?" is instilled in my head and is repeated on a daily basis because of you. Not only were you my first chef, but you taught me so much about life, food, and family. I'm honored to call you one of my best friends. Thank you for all you've done and thank you for your consistent motivation on a daily basis.

To Gary Danko, you were my first introduction into real food, a real chef's life, and you opened my eyes on how to be a real business operator. I can't thank you enough for taking me under your wing for so many years. I have nothing but love for you, sir.

To Miles Kunisaki, you are literally my hands and my feet. I couldn't have done it without you. Thank you for all your hard work and dedication. There's not a day I don't know how much you've given to me.

To my little brother Steven, who is way bigger (and by that I mean stronger. I know you thought I said you were fat, which you aren't) than me, my little sister Alexis, who is way better looking and stylish than me, and my older sister ☺ Chyllis, who is way smarter than me, I'm proud of who we've become, and I can't thank all of you enough for your support. I love you all.

To my core at Time Inc. Books, Betty Wong and Felicity Keane, boy, oh boy do I owe you two the world. I'm honored to have worked with both of you. Thank you for your long nights, many emails, and putting up with my OCD chef-ness. This book is as much me as it is the both of you.

To my literary agents, Jeff Kleinman and Claudia Cross, this book would not be real if it wasn't for your continuous telephone calls, your badgering me to write it, and your overall belief in me. ♡♡

And to Tamara Palmer, not bad for our first crack at a book, huh? Thank you, thank you, thank you for all your hard work.

Last, but not least, mucho names: Rick Hamer, Lynne Sloan, Tyler Nave, Tom Walton, Pumpkin and Teddy, Rachael Ray, Sunny Anderson, Pat Monahan, Hoda Kotb, Kathy Lee Gifford, Mara and Chris Padilla, Frank Stone, Bao Tonthat, Vanesa Sanchez, Jim Clarke, Chad Scott, Jackie Olensky, Nii-Ama Akuete, Rick Reichmuth, Lev Dagan, and Wes Romine aka Go Weser ☺.

XO,

METRIC EQUIVALENTS

The information in the following charts is provided to help cooks outside the United States successfully use the recipes in this book. All equivalents are approximate.

COOKING/OVEN TEMPERATURES

	Fahrenheit	Celsius	Gas Mark
Freeze Water	32° F	0° C	
Room Temp.	68° F	20° C	
Boil Water	212° F	100° C	
Bake	325° F	160° C	3
	350° F	180° C	4
	375° F	190° C	5
	400° F	200° C	6
	425° F	220° C	7
	450° F	230° C	8
Broil			Grill

LIQUID INGREDIENTS BY VOLUME

$1/4$ tsp	=					1 ml		
$1/2$ tsp	=					2 ml		
1 tsp	=					5 ml		
3 tsp	=	1 Tbsp	=	$1/2$ fl oz	=	15 ml		
2 Tbsp	=	$1/8$ cup	=	1 fl oz	=	30 ml		
4 Tbsp	=	$1/4$ cup	=	2 fl oz	=	60 ml		
$5^1/3$ Tbsp	=	$1/3$ cup	=	3 fl oz	=	80 ml		
8 Tbsp	=	$1/2$ cup	=	4 fl oz	=	120 ml		
$10^2/3$ Tbsp	=	$2/3$ cup	=	5 fl oz	=	160 ml		
12 Tbsp	=	$3/4$ cup	=	6 fl oz	=	180 ml		
16 Tbsp	=	1 cup	=	8 fl oz	=	240 ml		
1 pt	=	2 cups	=	16 fl oz	=	480 ml		
1 qt	=	4 cups	=	32 fl oz	=	960 ml		
				33 fl oz	=	1000 ml	=	1 l

(To convert ounces to grams, multiply the number of ounces by 30.)

1 oz	=	$1/16$ lb	=	30 g
4 oz	=	$1/4$ lb	=	120 g
8 oz	=	$1/2$ lb	=	240 g
12 oz	=	$3/4$ lb	=	360 g
16 oz	=	1 lb	=	480 g

EQUIVALENTS FOR DIFFERENT TYPES OF INGREDIENTS

Standard Cup	Fine Powder* (ex. flour)	Grain (ex. rice)	Granular (ex. sugar)	Liquid Solids (ex. butter)	Liquid (ex. milk)
1	120 g	150 g	190 g	200 g	240 ml
$3/4$	90 g	113 g	143 g	150 g	180 ml
$2/3$	80 g	100 g	125 g	133 g	160 ml
$1/2$	60 g	75 g	95 g	100 g	120 ml
$1/3$	40 g	50 g	63 g	67 g	80 ml
$1/4$	30 g	38 g	48 g	50 g	60 ml
$1/8$	15 g	19 g	24 g	25 g	30 ml

* Metrics based on King Arthur Flour.

LENGTH

(To convert inches to centimeters, multiply the number of inches by 2.5.)

1 in	=					2.5 cm		
6 in	=	$1/2$ ft			=	15 cm		
12 in	=	1 ft			=	30 cm		
36 in	=	3 ft	=	1 yd	=	90 cm		
40 in	=					100 cm	=	1m

INDEX

BLOOPER REEL